CHRISTIANITY

AND

MENTAL HEALTH

by

MAX LEACH

WM. C. BROWN COMPANY

Publishers

DUBUQUE, IOWA

dedicated

to

my wife who is my other self and my other hand

and

our children and their families who make our
lives so happily worth while.

Foreword

It is sincerely hoped that this book will be of some help and inspiration to those who read it.

Admittedly, it treats of an *ideal* way of life, the Christian way of life. God made the Christian way so that there might always be further steps for us to take. And each step that we take is a step toward better mental health.

My heartfelt thanks to my wife for her many hours of editorial work spent upon the manuscript, and all the many other helps she gave me; and my thanks to the many members of my classes in mental hygiene during the last five years who have patiently listened to parts of the manuscript and have encouraged its completion by their good response.

Remember, this is a human document, written by a human hand directed by a human brain. Only in the Truth from God are there no mistakes.

ML

Table of Contents

CHAPTER 1

Dynamics and Descriptions

One of the universal goals of man is happiness.

Happiness has been defined in many ways, but it takes more than a dictionary definition to tell really what happiness is. Happiness is a state of mind but is also a state of being and depends not only on self, but on others round about one. Happiness is an inner glow, an inner warmth. Happiness is a feeling of well-being. Happiness makes life worth the living and each day worth the effort and each night a time for welcome rest.

Happiness is an attitude that is a part of one's personality. Happiness is saying to oneself, and completely believing the statement: "I like what I am, who I am, what I'm doing, where I am. I like me, and the world that I'm in, and the things round about me. I like my family, and my friends, and even the strangers that I meet. Tomorrow and every tomorrow are going to be good days, and I'll like them too. I think that I would even like my enemies, if I had any."

Happiness, then, is not a fleeting and an evanescent something but instead is something that is a part of one, and is lasting.

True, no person is happy all the time. For the happiest, there come times of grief and pain and tears. But the basic pattern of the happy person's life is stable, and grief, pain and tears are but passing clouds in the steady brilliance of their day.

Man does much of what he does in the quest for happiness. Man steals, thinking that the possession of more money or things will make him happy. Man wars, thinking that the forceful subjugation of others will give him a security that leads to happiness. Man lies and cheats, thinking that easy short-cuts to some of the things he desires will make him happy. And man, being at the same time intelligent and ignorant, keeps on making the same old mistakes in the same old way with the same old results.

The psychotics and the neurotics are not happy people. The psychotic are those that in every-day language we call "crazy" and the neurotic are the ones we speak of as "highly nervous" or more correctly, "emotionally unstable." These are people whose mental health is very poor, and these are people who are miserable, unhappy, disturbed, upset, at odds with themselves, with their environment and with their position in time and space.

These are the people who are seeking for what they know not and what they cannot find, and in their abortive efforts to fool themselves and to fool others, they say things, do things, think things, and believe things that may fool themselves but certainly fool no one else for very long. These are the non-adjusted; these are the unhappy. Their number is legion.

It will be the persuasion of this book that a simple faith in Christianity as a way of life, believed in and *practiced*, will bring a high level of happiness, which is synonymous with good mental health, to the practicing believer. Not a selective belief and practice, not a half-hearted belief and practice, but a *whole* and a *whole-hearted* belief and practice.

For a better use of the pages of this book that follow, it is relevant to have some preliminary lessons in some of the simple facts relating to psychological processes and to mental health.

We largely react to life situations in the way we have been taught to react. Usually when we use the word "taught", we immediately think in terms of formal teaching, such as a teacher teaching arithmetic in the seventh grade. We need another concept than this, however, for most teaching is *not* formal teaching.

Why is a child afraid of the dark? Simply because he has been taught to be afraid of the dark. There is nothing in the dark that will hurt one, if one manifests reasonable care in the way one gets around. It has been conclusively proved that there is no instinct within people to cause them to be afraid of the dark. We no longer believe in ghosts, demons, evil spirits, witches, and bogeymen that come flittering out when the shades of night have fallen. How, then, does a child go about getting taught to be afraid of the dark?

There are many ways. One of the simplest, and one of the most common, is for the infant to learn to associate the dark with insecurity. If the unhappy, hungry, sick, upset baby is regularly left in the dark just with his own self and his own misery, he may come to associate these constant feelings with the dark and may be conditioned all of his life to have a strong emotional reaction in connection with the dark that we speak of as "fear." But since there is no instinctive fear of the dark for the infant, if his association with darkness is usually in connection with pleasant feelings, drowsiness, a full stomach, a sense of security in feeling rather than knowing that he has been born into a world of love— if his bed is comfortable, his clothes dry, his stomach full of milk, his head full of sleep, and his heart full of security—

then the dark will not be something of insecurity but rather something that is soft and warm and comforting. This child will likely never be very afraid of the dark.

There are other ways, of course, whereby the child is taught to fear the dark. As he grows old enough to understand, he may see others about him who are afraid of the dark. The average child has all the intelligence that he needs —and it is not long until he has *learned* from these others the feeling of fear of the dark, although he could not under any circumstances tell you why he feels that way.

Then later he may learn through words that the dark is a fearsome something. Other children and sometimes even adults tell him scary stories connected with the dark. Sometimes by word they show their fear: "I don't want to go in there; it's dark." It is true that this kind of fear of the dark is a more superficial thing than the feelings of fear that one absorbs, and usually does not go very deep nor last very long. Even at a later stage many of us like to be scared by making midnight excursions to haunted houses or graveyards, or meeting in some secluded spot and telling scary stories.

Here we have examined an area of learning that may be strong enough in some of us to interfere in small measure with our happiness—and we can see that it has not been taught in any very formal manner. But this part of a personality, this part of a life pattern, has been learned, and thoroughly learned.

So it will be a basic assumption of this book that many, if not most, of those things relating to our happiness and mental health, are learned. And what can be learned can be unlearned—although strangely, it is sometimes more difficult to unlearn than to learn.

Consequently the human being does not *have* to remain in his rut of ignorance or fear or improper action. He can learn better if so he will. He can achieve a position a little lower than the angels—if he is willing to do some unlearning along with his learning. It is no accident that Christianity is a teaching religion; it is no coincidence that Christ told his disciples to go into all the world and teach.

It may not be correct to say that all unhappy people are neurotic, but it certainly is correct to say that all neurotic people are unhappy.

It is true that many neurotic people are so disturbed that in their frantic casting about to find happiness they sometimes do outstanding pieces of work in the world; nevertheless it is very doubtful that they find happiness in the doing of this work.

It is by no means true that people who do great works in the world are universally neurotic. Some of the greatest of our Americans have been well-adjusted and happy people and have done their great work simply as the routine part of a great life. But there are many other great ones who have done great works as a product of their disordered lives, and found no real happiness therein.

Neurotic behavior has been rather thoroughly classified by the writers in the field.

One of the most common of all neurotic behavior patterns is the anxiety complex, and one probably will not have to go outside of his own residential block to find a number of sufferers from this neurotic complaint.

The neurotic with the anxiety complex is the chronic worrier. Actually this person is always afraid, and he does not know of what, nor why; he only knows he is afraid.

It is true, of course, that this fear will attach to anything. The worriers will be afraid of polio during the polio season and afraid of flu during the flu season. They will be afraid of depressions during good times and worse times during bad times. They will be afraid of the H bombs, subversives that can't be recognized, losing their jobs, the house burning down, burglars, mad dogs, electrocution from electric wiring, falling airplanes and so on through a lifetime. At any given time, of course, they can tell you what they are afraid of—but actually, they are just afraid, period. Since no one likes to say simply: "I'm afraid," then they must attach their fear to something to appear rational.

These are neurotics, you ask?

Yes, these are neurotics. They are less efficient than they would otherwise be; they are unhappy; they are disturbed; they waste much of their life's energy in unproductive ways. Thus neuroticism is constituted.

Then why are there so many of these neurotics whose symptom is the anxiety complex?

There are good reasons why.

These reasons are what we technically speak of as the dynamics of behavior.

Go back to the child who has learned to be afraid of the dark, even long before he can speak or understand spoken language. This child has come to associate darkness with all his feelings of insecurity, and fear and a feeling of insecurity are very much alike. This child's feelings of insecurity do not attach only to darkness, because after all, it is not the darkness that has caused the child to feel insecure, but his whole life situation. And almost without exception, this same life situation will be about as insecure in the light as in the dark. Now if during the first year of life of this child, most of his feelings—and feelings are our most powerful memories—are of an unpleasant, fearful, insecure tone, then we can safely assume that the world, for him, has taken on this same coloration. And if the first six years of life of this child are built on such a basis, it will be fortunate if this child as an adolescent or an adult has no more severe neurosis than an anxiety complex.

Again, like the child who learned to fear the dark, there are many other ways wherein anxiety complexes are begun and nurtured to full size.

A child may come along through the first years of childhood and youth with his life built on a good, stable, emotional base. Then, during the time that he still looks to Mamma and Daddy to meet most of his needs in the world, the misfortunes of life that are common to all strike his family. Mother and Dad, being concerned about their family's welfare, are worried sick for a period of time because of the outlook. The smaller child, who reacts emotionally with many times more power than his mother and dad, immediately reacts to the whole atmosphere—and a few weeks, or months, of such an atmosphere may leave the child with the beginnings of a real anxiety complex.

But do anxiety complexes begin only in childhood?

The answer is definitely no.

Although it is quite difficult for the adult who has lived through childhood and youth and adolescence in a good, happy, friendly world to develop an anxiety complex, it can be done.

If, as adults, they set unrealistic goals, or they are too sensitive to the pressure of the times and the people, or they have little faith either in themselves or others or God, or they are constantly failures in their own eyes because they do not measure up to the standards of those round about them—and for many other reasons—the adult can develop a first-class anxiety complex.

Probably most anxiety complexes are developed after adulthood, or at least adolescence, has been reached. It is the common neurosis of the American people. If statistics could be compiled, they would likely show that it is one of the most costly neuroses.

Regardless of how it has developed, it can be abolished.

Almost as common among neurotic complaints as anxiety is neurasthenia. Or to say it more simply, emotional fatigue and exhaustion.

Neurasthenia is the feeling of tiredness, apathy, lack of ambition, that comes about from emotional causes. It can be very devastating in its effects, because the neurasthenic is quite often too fatigued to do anything that would make life more livable for himself and those round about him except the most necessary things; and he performs these necessities with no graciousness and no measure of joy. Hardly anything stimulates him to pleasurable anticipation, and life stays flat, monotonous, colorless.

In popular articles of late, neurasthenia has been called the "housewife's complaint." Supposedly it is much more common among the keeper-at-home than amongst those who work away from home. Such a conclusion may be doubtful. Those who work among a large number of other people are more or less forced to hide the way they feel and to perform their job creditably in spite of their feelings if they want to keep their job. The housewife is in a perfect milieu for letting her feelings get the best of her, with her children and husband sometimes in the role of catching whatever she pitches.

The usual reason assigned for the "housewife's complaint" is that fundamentally she resents the role which she has chosen for herself. She wants to eat her cake and have it too. She wants to be a glamour girl as well as the steady, dependable wife and mother. She may want to be the right hand of a business tycoon and at the same time want to be the hand that rocks the cradle. She may feel that her personality, brains, and energy are all being wasted on a dreadful treadmill of diets, dishes, and diapers.

It would be impossible for persons to be neurasthenics because of the work they do if they thought this work the most interesting, the most challenging, the most productive of any work that they might do.

No housewife would ever have "housewife's complaint" if she could but recognize that she certainly has the most challenging and most productive job on earth, and at least in some respects the most interesting. Possibly our social times can take a large share of the blame for not giving the wife and mother more credit and more praise than is given. Few of the outstanding personalities of the newspapers and magazines of today are outstanding because they have made such a success of being home-bodies.

The causes for neurasthenia are legion—but contentment is never one of the causes.

Whatever the causes, it is no longer theory but fact that our emotional state can be tremendously important to our physical state. Continued neurasthenic states can lead to impaired body tone and functioning; digestive, circulatory, and possibly respiratory disorders. Since a normal sex life is part and parcel of a normal home life for a husband and wife, one of the first areas where neurasthenia may take its insinuating grip is in the sexual area.

Hysteria is the technical name for one of the most unusual of the severe neuroses. This is not to be confused with the phenomenon of the person who laughs so long and so hard that he begins to cry, and the crying gets out of control. We say this person is hysterical, but remember that he is not suffering from hysteria.

In the neurosis that we call hysteria some very peculiar things happen. The victim may become blind or deaf or dumb or paralyzed. He may lose complete feeling in portions of his body; or he may have strange tingling sensations in places, quite often in the extremities. These symptoms are what are called conversion symptoms, since they represent a conversion of deep feeling into bodily response, or lack of response.

A reasonably common hysterical symptom is the loss of one's voice. After thorough medical examinations it may be found that there is nothing physically wrong with the patient's voice, throat, or lung mechanisms. But he can't talk.

Investigation will prove that within this patient's life there is some tremendously moving threat, or fear, or disturbance—that one way of escaping this catastrophe is to be voiceless. Of course the patient does not reason in this way, and thus make-believe that he is voiceless. It is more as if he is hypnotized from down deep within himself; he actually cannot talk. Sometimes such patients regain their voices when the catastrophe that is threatening is removed. Sometimes they do not. It has been shown that hysterics, while hypnotized, do regain the use of the faculty that they have lost, proving that their symptom is from a psychological and not a physical source.

Probably there are many more people suffering from hysterical symptoms than we dream. It is very likely that most of the so-called faith cures of the present day are cures effected on hysterics. Since their ailment is not of the body but of the mind, it follows that if they believe they are cured, they are.

Possibly all of us at one time or another give in to a diminutive form of hysteria. Escaping from almost any difficult situation through bodily disturbance is certainly a conversion symptom. A splitting headache that keeps us from meeting an undesirable appointment is one of the most common of conversion symptoms.

Physicians say that more than half of all the patients they see are suffering psychologically rather than physiologically.

The world is full of the chronically ill, hypochondriacs, ailers. For many of these people their illness and their symptoms serve a purpose even though the one afflicted may be unconscious of the purpose served.

Truly here is a great area of neuroticism.

It is standard practice in any discussion of the neuroses to include obsessions, compulsions, manias, and phobias. Another that we shall discuss in this book is rigidity of adjustment. The neurotic, whatever his brand, is nearly always emotionally inflexible. He cannot adjust his emotions to fit the situation but must always try to make the situation fit his emotions. But more about this rigidity and inflexibility later.

An obsession is a fixed idea.

And this is a form of neuroticism, you ask? Indeed it is.

One of the very common obsessions among adults is the idea that a certain food does not agree with one. It is true of course that when a person having this obsession does eat the food which the obsession concerns, then the person likely will have all the symptoms of a food upset. He may have cramps, or nausea, or headache, or whatever. And there is no doubt that the cramps, nausea, and headache hurt just as severely as if the food did poison him in some way. Just because a bodily pain has a psychological beginning is no reason to believe that it is any less severe than other pains.

The reasons why one can have an obsession about food are numerous. It may be he does not like the food, but feeling it would be somewhat childish to say: "I don't like that," he covers up his real reasons, both for himself and others, and finds that the food "doesn't agree with him." It may be that at some time he ate too much of this food and had some very unpleasant experiences in connection with the ailment. And since, he has kept this emotional memory of this circumstance and applied it even to the very mention of the food; naturally, he would insist the food doesn't agree with him. Or it may be that this person, again as a child, has simply adopted the attitude and feeling of this food from some adult close to him.

All of us at one time or another have had mild obsessions, and they are no sign at all that we are near neurotic, or that we are well on the road to getting that way. Have you ever awakened in the middle of the night with a song running through your mind? This is a mild obsession, the kind that everyone will have now and then. Or have you ever started on a trip, and although you very carefully checked everything before you left, were tortured for hours, or maybe days, with the certainty that you left a window up, or the water on, or the cat in?

Obsessions of course can run the full scale to the most absurd and extreme. In a paranoid psychosis for instance, one may be completely and wholly obsessed with the idea that he is infallible, with no possibility existing that he could ever be wrong. When obsessions become fixed and operate in some extreme way such as this, we usually speak of them as delusions.

From this brief discussion of obsessions, it can be easily seen that overdone they can be rather severe neurotic symptoms. But another fact emerges as well—that the normal person may have occasional mild symptoms of neurotic behavior that do not at all mark him as neurotic. The true neurotic has incorporated his neurotic symptoms into his personality pattern and again manifests very rigid behavior in holding to them and resisting their being torn away from him.

A compulsion is simply an obsession translated into action.

If, instead of an idea or a thought or a feeling, the strong and persistent fixity is an action, then we have a compulsion.

As a child, a boy was playing with a group of his friends in an old oil warehouse. The floor was rough and splintery, a real hazard even to feet as tough as his were. The boys had begun their play wearing their shoes, but during the violence of the action, this particular lad had lost one of his. Another boy noticed the loss and said, "You'd better put your shoe on; don't you know that one shoe off and one shoe on is bad luck?" The boy did not know and did not believe it; so he left the shoe off. Within five minutes he had run a tremendous splinter into his bare foot to such an extent that one of the boys had to take a pair of pliers to pull it out. It was extremely painful and made a tremendous emotional impact upon him. And since emotions are the strongest memories, for years—yes, years—afterwards, he would no more have one shoe on and one off than he would put scorpions down his own back. This was an obsession in action, thus a compulsion.

Although today he feels reasonably comfortable with one shoe on and one shoe off, he is never in such a comfortable situation but that he remembers his compulsion of years ago.

On another occasion this child remembers picnicking with his father and mother and two friends of theirs. They had gone hill climbing and on the way down his mother's friend began descending too fast and fell, raking all the skin off one side of her face. The pain and the fright made her almost hysterical, and she really had a small-sized case of the screaming-meemies. Through her sobs and screams she kept repeating, "I knew I should have picked up that pin this morning; I knew it, I knew it." When the tumult and the shouting had died enough for the boy to get his mother's attention—and he was really upset about the whole matter— he asked her what the woman meant. She said, "There's an old saying that if you 'see a pin and pick it up, all the day you'll have good luck; but see a pin and let it lie, to good luck you'll say good-bye!' "

This made such a strong emotional impression on him that for years he felt compelled to pick up any loose pin wherever he saw it lying. Time has loosened the power of this compulsion on him also.

Again, such compulsions as these are fairly common and do not brand one as being truly neurotic. But look for a minute at some of the compulsions that the truly neurotic have.

One young man had a compulsion to write notes. When he was having some of his worst emotional trouble, he would get up in the night and write a note; he would stop his car on the way to school and write a note. He had his pockets stuffed with notes, his pocketbook crammed with notes. He wrote so many notes that he was upset by his note writing compulsion, and his wife was more than upset.

To oversimplify the reasons why he wrote notes to himself, he was having emotional trouble connected with his own opinion of himself, and the note writing helped give him both a release and served somewhat in the stead of doing the things that he really felt that he must do but didn't. In some way the notes were a promise to himself that he would be better and do better; and because he was so mixed up in his emotional life, he was compelled to write the notes in order to keep living with himself.

Then another young man had a compulsion in regard to the asphalt tile laid in the recreation room of a college dormitory. When he went into this particular room he said it nearly drove him crazy—that he could not walk in the room without feeling compelled always to step in the middle of each tile, never stepping on one of the cracks.

The reasons, as they developed, make sense. This particular boy had very strong homosexual urges and had made a few homesexual contacts. Aside from this he was a very moral young man; in fact, in the public eye he was a very religious young man. Without any doubt he had severe feelings of guilt about his homosexual urges and contacts without having taken any positive steps towards alleviating the situation. Consequently his compulsion to control his behavior in regard to the asphalt tiles gave him a feeling of mastery over himself that was completely spurious, of course —and too, he had heard the old childhood rhyme—"Step on a crack, and break your mother's back." And since mothers and fathers have a very prominent place in the homosexual's warp and woof, it was no psychological accident that this boy chose this particular thing for his compulsion.

One ex-psychotic had a very difficult time doing the ordinary, everyday things that he wanted to do if he were to be recognized again as a normal person. One year he did enroll in some college classes as an auditor; but every day it was a struggle for him to get up, get dressed, eat some food, be on his way. Quite frequently he would miss the class altogether, and one day he told why. He had a negative compulsion—in order to leave his room, he had to turn off the light, which was operated by a pull cord switch. On those days when his compulsion was operating, he could *not* turn off his light. He would try, would even get his hands on the pull cord, but could not pull it. Naturally if he could not turn off the light, he could not leave the room. And if he could not leave the room, he could not get out into the swing of things.

Compulsions invariably serve some need, obscure though it be.

Another of the curious manifestations of the neurotic is the phobia; a phobia is defined as a strong and irrational fear.

We do not consider it neurotic to be afraid of water when the boat turns over, or to be afraid of fire when you waken in the middle of the night and smell smoke, or to be afraid of snakes when you see a rattler in the path in front of you. These fears are part of God's built-in way to help us preserve our lives.

But to be deathly afraid of bones, or of a small room, or of water in a bath tub—and to be so afraid of them that they cause us to act peculiarly—under such circumstances then we can be sure that we are dealing with a true phobia.

"Was any one ever afraid of bones?" you might ask.

Here is a case of a true bone-phobia.

This phobic was a young man; he was taking a general psychology course when he came to a counselor about his phobia. He explained that he could not take a physiology course at all because of having to work with various skeletons. He would be trembling and weak, break out in a cold sweat, and even feel as though he were going to have convulsions if he had to get too close to the bones. He was especially upset if the skeletons had the jaws and teeth intact.

In attempting to find out why he had this phobia, he and the counselor covered the following: as a child, he was under rather careful control by his mother, and he was kept close at home in the yard. He could remember that when he was three or four years old he heard the older folks tell some rather frightening tales, and he recalled that some of them dealt with dogs.

One day he was feeling very Columbus-like; so he opened the yard gate and ambled down the street. He was about a block from home when suddenly coming toward him was the largest dog he had ever seen. This would not have been so bad, except that the dog had a great bone in his mouth, and on this bone were left a few shreds of meat. The young man, in later description of the incident, could vividly remember his belief that the flesh on the bone in the dog's mouth moved, and he was nearly frightened senseless. He could not remember much about getting back home, but he did recall that during the night he was awakened in the middle of a nightmare, and there in a moonlit patch of floor he again saw the bone with the moving flesh on it. This scared him even worse than the actual seeing of the dog and the bone.

Since that time until just recently the young man has had a phobia concerning bones, and especially bones with teeth in them.

Sometimes phobias are representations of the general fears that a person possesses, but they attach themselves to some specific object or situation.

There is the example of a neurotic who had made his life just one big mess of fears. He was afraid that he couldn't make a living for his family, that his wife would leave him, and finally that he had committed the unpardonable sin. Part of his fears concentrated into a phobia relating to going higher than the second story of any building. He would go to the second floor but no higher, regardless of the circumstances.

In searching for causes for this particular phobia, it developed that this fear was simply a representation of all the fear that this man had, and was not related to any specific learning situation as was the phobia concerning bones.

Manias are extreme compulsions, usually of such a nature as to be quite socially unacceptable, and that draw disfavor down upon the possessor of the mania. Maniac is a common term for the violently crazy, although the possessor of a mania is an overdone neurotic. It is apropos at this time to suggest that some of the bad neuroses are actually more incapacitating than a mild psychosis.

The kleptomaniac has the compulsion to steal; the pyro-maniac has the compulsion to set fires—always to houses or buildings, not just to piles of paper or wood. It is thought by most psychologists that there is always a sexual component in the dynamics of the manias; in general this seems to be true, although it is not likely to be true without exception.

The most noted and publicized of the manias is that which moves its possessor to the commission of sexual per-versions, usually of a criminal nature. Thus the compulsive homosexual attempts to seduce the minor boy (most of these cases involve men and boys) or the criminal pervert sexually attacks an infant or a small child, with death oftentimes in-tervening. These people are usually not classified as insane before the law, but they are much more dangerous to society than many who are.

Such a classification of the neuroses does not take in the waves and cross currents and rip tides of neurotic behavior that at some time or another in life assail every person.

When a series of minor misfortunes hit on top of a bad cold and the loss of two nights' sleep, almost any normal human being will act like a neurotic.

He may snarl at everything and anybody, may become angered over virtually nothing, may take offense at what was intended for a compliment but he interprets as an insult. He may be nervous and jumpy and in such a state of mind, emo-tion, and body that life, at the time, simply isn't worth living. For the time being, this one is definitely a neurotic.

It happens to the best of us.

But the normal person has the reserves, the intelligence, the fundamental emotional stability so that this is only a passing squall on a usually calm harbor. Under no circumstances can this person be classified as a neurotic, even though for a short time he may be more neurotic than the best—or worst.

The true neurotic is always just outside the eye of an emotional hurricane.

Very briefly we should consider the psychoses, or in non-technical language, those who are classified as "crazy."

The usual glib definition of the psychotic is that he is one who has lost touch with reality. The facts are, however, that no living person ever loses touch with all reality, no matter how disturbed this one might be. And who is to say correctly that the one who really believes he is Julius Caesar is any farther away from reality than the one who thinks real happiness can be bought?

Society says so, but how correctly is not yet determined.

It is a maxim of psychology that the kind of psychosis one has is determined by the basic personality of the psychotic. By this it is simply meant that the personality before a person becomes a psychotic determines what kind of a psychotic he will be.

In every day language we many times speak of a person "going crazy." We are smarter than we think. This is exactly what happens. No one was ever born crazy, nor no one ever will be. And as we are at last at the point where we can collect evidence concerning psychological matters and assess it scientifically, we are becoming more and more sure that no one, when born, is fated or pre-determined to "go crazy."

It is true that certain diseases, certain chemical poisons, certain bodily injuries under certain circumstances cause one to have all the symptoms of a psychosis. These can be read-ily determined, however, as being symptoms of the aforemen-tioned causes. The ordinary psychoses are spoken of as being functional, and by this is meant that they are a product of functioning—in other words, because of one's experiences and selective responses, one takes the path to sanity or insanity.

Some of the various forms of psychotic behavior have been classified and named; however, it is all too true that there is much overlapping of behavior patterns—and it is on the basis of these behavior patterns only that a classification can be made—and that many times psychologists and psy-chiatrists who have been in the business for a long time can-not fully agree on a specific diagnosis.

One of the most common of the psychoses is schizo-phrenia. This particular form of mental illness was first la-beled dementia praecox, or freely translated "precocious de-mentia." It was so called because of the high incidence of people between the ages of fifteen and thirty-five who suf-fered from the disease, in contrast to the more commonly known senile dementias, or mental disorders of old age. It is not digressing too far at this time to make this statement: a person is *not* fated to become demented, crazy, or queer, just because he gets old.

Schizophrenia is marked by what seems to be a splitting of the personality. A mild schizophrenic may get along very well and act very normally in most situations, but in others he may be completely out of touch with reality. One schizo-phrenic that was observed by a class of mental hygiene stu-dents was very neatly dressed, completely oriented as to time, place, name, and the other basic trivia of life—but during the observation he grabbed his abdomen as if in great misery, and said: "there it goes." The young physician by his side said, "There what goes?" very well knowing the coming answer.

"My stomach," the patient said, acting as though he were in great misery, as indeed he was; "it just flew out the window," and for five minutes the patient suffered just as one might suffer if he had no stomach.

But all of a sudden his face brightened up, and he said, "I'm all right now, it's back." And again he was quite normal in most of the affairs of the everyday world.

Schizophrenics are usually sub-classified according to symptoms. The hebephrenic is the schizophrenic that is happy, regardless. The news of a horrible accident to loved ones sends him into spasms of laughter.

The catatonic is the schizophrenic that takes some rigid posture, or else is so flexible that he keeps his bodily appendages in any position one might place them—and at the same time seems to be completely withdrawn from all contact with the world, not talking, not eating, not functioning normally in any way. It has been shown, however, that the catatonic is very conscious of what transpires around him, even though he seems not to be.

The paranoid schizophrenic shows the ordinary signs of schizophrenia along with strong delusions of persecution; these delusions usually become hallucinations. The patient hears voices, sees handwriting on the wall, or lurking figures that may be waiting and plotting.

The simple schizophrenic may show almost any kind of a symptom that indicates he is "out of touch."

In all psychoses there is disordered affect. By this is simply meant that one's emotions, or "feelings" are out of kilter, and do not function normally.

"Certainly," you say; "it doesn't take a psychologist to see that a psychotic is not emotionally balanced."

Actually psychoses and neuroses are much more emotional illnesses than they are mental illnesses. Some psychotics can do a wonderful mental job in all areas except where their feelings are out of order. Then no amount of reason, persuasion, or logic will touch them.

Another of the common kinds of psychotics is the depressive. This is the person that has such long fits of depression that he becomes completely incapacitated for any of the ordinary activities of everyday life. A feeling of depression is clearly an emotion, but this emotion becomes so strong that the mental processes of the depressive do become disordered; and again in any area touching on or near his affective state, he cannot think clearly. Reason or logic does not touch him. Nothing can be more futile than to try to convince a depressive, through reason, that he should not worry.

Opposite the depressives on the psychotic scale are the manics. These are the persons whose emotions are disturbed as severely as the depressives', but their disorder of affect shows up in that they are highly excited and excitable, forever moving, talking, laughing—and their thought processes move so rapidly and incoherently that they may make little or no sense in their talking; they may jump from the middle of one topic to another, and their attention is easily caught, but may not be so easily held. These are some of the superficial symptoms.

They may laugh a great deal; manic psychotic laughter brings forcibly to consciousness the origin of the expression, "He laughs like a maniac."

Whereas the violently depressed may be dangerous to himself because of suicidal tendencies, the violently manic may be dangerous to others because he may have all kinds of delusions and hallucinations.

The other major classification of psychotics is labeled paranoia. Paranoia is a little like, but considerably different from paranoid schizophrenia. Whereas the true schizophrenic will nearly always have hallucinations, the paranoid is characterized usually by a strong delusional system; and as a rule this system causes the paranoid to believe he is violently persecuted, or hated, or else makes him believe that he is grander than any other human ever was or will be. Because of these feelings, the paranoid may be very dangerous and aggressive, although not always so, and not every paranoid is so. Probably there are more true paranoids living among us today that are not classified as "insane" than any of the other types of psychotics, simply because in their delusional system they can support it with such logic and persuasion that many sane people are made to believe in their delusions. And as paranoids as a class are nearly always intelligent persons, this makes it even more difficult for the average person to spot them as psychotic.

One of the most unusual of the groups of mentally ill are those that are classified as psychopathic personalities.

These are the people who commit anti-social acts with little or no feeling of conscience or remorse. The three kinds of anti-social actions they indulge in have to do with lying, stealing, and sex offenses. The things they do are not compulsions in the sense that the stealing of a kleptomaniac is a compulsion; in stealing and lying they obviously fill some need of themselves—and this is true of course in a different sense in sex offenses. They can be quite canny in their commission of the offense, or it may be blatant and public. But the common thread of the psychopathic personalities is that they do not have feelings concerning the act that could at all be classified as normal. If caught, say, in a stealing offense, they may show every sign of remorse; but within minutes after being freed, may be back at their stealing again.

For a long time psychologists could come up with no better explanation of their activity than that something was left out of them at birth that had to do with moral development, and thus they once were called psychopathic constitutional inferiors. A more widely accepted viewpoint at the present time is that they are taught to have no conscience; by their life experiences and through family attitudes they are actually trained not to have the same moral outlooks and attitudes that most of us seem to absorb in the early years of our lives.

Thus we find a brief description of the more common of the classifications of the mentally and emotionally ill. There are many others that have names, but in some measure they probably overlap into these that have been discussed.

Do not make the mistake of thinking that mental or emotional illnesses run an exact parallel to physical illnesses. They do not.

A physical illness is caused by germs or bodily malfunctioning or unbalance of some kind. Usually the reasons for the illness can be identified and a proper course of treatment prescribed.

But a mental or emotional illness has no one cause such as a physical illness and many times cannot be readily diagnosed other than to say, "That fellow is in bad shape". Mental and emotional illnesses are a part of one's personality;

physical illnesses are superimposed on one. Physical illlnesses, if they are germ caused, are caught. Mental and emotional illnesses are developed as the result of learning experiences, thus also in a sense are caught.

The psychologist and the psychiatrist, who are professionally trained to work with the mentally and emotionally disturbed, can do much in the attack upon this problem, but the solution of the whole matter is by no means in their hands.

The roots of mental illness always have their beginnings in the home, with the great growth of this noxious plant all too often watered and fertilized by the social environment.

And here is where Christianity, believed, applied, and practiced, can strike the telling blow. For Christianity teaches the best person-to-person relationships and the best personal-social relationships.

Since mental illness functions only in relation to others, good mental health is axiomatic when one's relationships with others are right.

Christianity, if believed and practiced, makes these relationships right.

Therefore Christianity, if believed and practiced, makes for good mental health.

CHAPTER II

Security

One of the strongest psychological needs of all of us is the need for security.

This world at its very best is an insecure place. In sub-human life we find that it is a law of nature that one plant or animal may use another plant or animal as food; although at the human level we do not have any exactly parallel conditions existing in the present day world. Nevertheless we do find that man poses a great threat to his fellow man in various ways.

In addition many people are worried about where their next meal will come from, how they will buy the clothes that they need, where they will get the adequate shelter that they feel that they must have—and besides these very understandable thoughts and feelings concerning needs, there are those who worry about many other things. With all of the reasons indicating that he is insecure, man caps the whole thing off with a basic feeling of insecurity concerning life itself.

For the Christian who really believes that Christ's teachings are divine and thus true, this last fear, this last capstone of insecurity, ceases to exist. For this person death is not an ending but a beginning. For this person life is not too severe in its offering, because whatever might be the lacks and short-comings of this person, the worst that life can offer is death; and since death itself is not bad but good from the Christian viewpoint, such an outlook does not bring with it feelings of insecurity.

No one knows just how much this fundamental and usually subconscious fear of the end of this life may have to do with his personality. We recognize, of course, that in every person there is the built-in reaction against imminent death in a physical way. By this is meant that if a person is thrown into the water and feels that he is drowning he will struggle to survive; if he feels himself falling he will clutch at anything that might offer him support and will hold him up. Although we recognize that this is a part of every person, nevertheless there is no reason to believe that this natural holding to life of itself causes feelings of insecurity.

Man is unusual in many ways, but one of the most unusual is that he recognizes the coming of his own death. Even the small child is soon accustomed to the idea of death, and possibly even to the sight of death. As man grows older, he cannot help but know that with the passing of time death comes much nearer. When one reaches middle age and goes on into old age, if he is thinking and does not hide the facts from himself, he recognizes that physically he dies a little each day. But even such an idea as this should not be too disturbing because it puts death in the light of being a function of life and not necessarily an abrupt ending. However, no man-made philosophy or logic has been able to give man the feeling of security that he would like to have in the face of his knowledge of death. He must have something else to give him real security besides this knowledge.

Like any one else the Christian can see the inexorable march of time; each day is a part of the orderly, planned process from the unknown to the unknown. But for him the end of this march is not a great question mark; instead it is only a part, a great part, of the whole orderly process. To him his personality does not cease to exist, and life is not cut off from him but instead is only made richer and fuller. So for the Christian the contemplation of death is not a disconcerting thing but a stabilizing thing. For the Christian death is not defeat but victory. "I tell you this, brethren: flesh and blood cannot inherit the kingdom of God, nor does the perishable inherit the imperishable. Lo! I tell you a mystery. We shall not all sleep, but we shall all be changed, in a moment, in the twinkling of an eye, at the last trumpet. For the trumpet will sound, and the dead will be raised imperishable, and we shall be changed. For this perishable nature must put on the imperishable, and this mortal nature must put on immortality. When the perishable puts on the imperishable, and the mortal puts on immortality, then shall come to pass the saying that is written: 'Death is swallowed up in victory. O death, where is thy victory? O death, where is thy sting?'" These words are found in first Corinthians, fifteen.

Although scoffers may laugh and may provoke the Christian to try to prove the basis of his faith, the very fact that he cannot prove it through his own experience makes his security all the stronger in the face of the invincible march of coming death. Even though the scoffer may laugh, it is an uneasy laugh; although he may scorn, his scorn is tinged with fear. Possibly the Christian cannot explain to those who do not believe as he believes; but within himself is the truth of his own faith and his own belief. Real, solid security—he lives in a world that is not a threatening world; he lives in a world that is a means to an end and that gives him an opportunity to make his life rich and sure, a pattern complete, perfect, and whole.

Then it may be possible that people who do not have the Christian outlook may have a basic insecurity that begins with an unconscious, or even conscious, fear of death. For the shaky and trembling base of this person, the Christian has substituted a solid and a firm base of real security upon which he can build and build for that which will last forever.

Most adults in America today believe that security lies in the material things of this life. First on the list, of course, is money. There is no denying—money can be converted into power, into food, into shelter, into entertainment, into many of the things that the world puts great store by. Because money can actually be converted into all of these things, then money itself has come to have a great and a deep symbolism for most people. The advertisements in our magazines speak of security in terms of money saved up in some form. The average outlook of the average person transferred to the average child is that success and security come with the making and amassing of sizable amounts of money. As a result and because of the very tangible nature of the things that money can bring one, most adults have come to think much more about worldly security than about any security of any other kind. Actually this is an implied admission that they do not think much of a future life. Although many may give lip service to such an idea, they do not really and basically believe that there is any such thing as a future life. They will glibly admit that you can't take it with you; nevertheless they vie just as vigorously with one another to get more of it, whether to spend immediately, or to save and spend at some later date, or just to have a lot of it as a symbol of security. Many things are done in this struggle for gaining momentary security; many good, many bad. In his fight to get more of this stuff, a man can justify the doing of almost anything. This of course is no new thing, for since man has been on the earth many men have believed that the end justifies the means.

Occasionally however, man's faith in the security of money and the other kinds of things that money can bring is shaken. The beginning of the depression of the 30's made many persons living today understand that there is no real security in money as such. Banks failed; stocks became worthless. However, in lush times, many forget.

If one can stand off and be somewhat objective about this, he sees that actually the man who chases money as security is chasing a will-o-the-wisp. For if money actually brings security, or the feeling of security which is the real thing being sought, then the person who has achieved the amassing of money or is in the process of doing so should be a person who enjoys good, if not nearly perfect, mental hygiene. Just one swift look around indicates that this is not so.

The man who chases money gets both the money and ulcers. When he gets the money he is hardly ever content with what he has, but he wants that much more. And so on ad infinitum. After he has made it he wonders what to do with it; whether to make this investment or that; whether or not this place to put it is safe or unsafe. He is always suspicious of his fellowman, because he is sure that his fellowman knows that he has this money and is after part of it by foul means or fair. Since he knows how many tangible things it will buy, he must of necessity be made somewhat selfish, because it will take a certain amount to keep him in the things that he must have throughout his life, and there may not be enough to share with someone else, even though this someone else may be near and dear to him—although not so dear as the money and what it represents. So the chasing of the money itself may keep one in a state of tension and may cause some unpleasant things to happen. After he gets what seems to be a reasonable amount stored up and away, he quite often does not manifest the serene countenance that comes from a foundation of good mental health, but he seems to be just as afraid of as many things as his brother who has not nearly so much as he. Hydrogen bombs, disease germs, highway accidents, and any and all of the bodily ills that may beset one add to his insecurity. Although he has feelings of confidence in the fact that money will buy the very best of medical attention, still, if he is honest with himself, he admits that the very best of medical attention will not make his body go on forever. His money cannot ward off the inevitable approach of old age. Poor or rich, black or white, he sees the result of the years in his diminished bodily activity just as surely as if there were no money in the world. So for this person, it is somewhat tragic that this in which he places his faith stealthily and inevitably proves that it is not worthy of his faith.

For the Christian who believes in Christian principles and teachings and ethics as his way of life, and a highway to another life, is not beset by one of the things that besets his money-seeking brother. He is content to make a reasonable living for himself and those that depend upon him. He is content with what he has. He suffers under no illusions that much money will ward off the evils of this world and of the flesh that are common to all men. He can take money or leave it. And with the taking or the leaving his mental hygiene is good and his actions are usually correct; correct at least from the viewpoint of the effect it has upon him and on those around him. From a strictly cold business viewpoint he may act very foolishly. This man like his brother who is seeking money as security has established a set of values; although there is no tangible symbol of his set of values, and he has nothing that he can convert immediately into things of the flesh and of the world. Nevertheless he does have that which is valuable to him and which is unchanged. It is not merely unchanging, however; because the longer he believes in his security as coming through the Christian Way, the more valuable it becomes to him. He becomes more content, more serene, more at peace. And make no mistake—this is not merely a lifeless, supine contentment, but this is a man or a woman vigorous, alive, living, loving to the fullest extent of his capacities.

For many, food comes to be both a symbol and a substance of security. Certainly the Christian body as well as the non-Christian body must alike have food for its well being. But the Christian has a very special instruction from his teacher in regard to this. "Therefore I tell you, do not be anxious about your life, what you shall eat or what you shall drink, nor about your body, what you shall put on. Is not life more than food, and the body more than clothing? Look at the birds of the air: they neither sow nor reap nor gather into barns, and yet your heavenly Father feeds them. Are you not of more value than they?" These are Christ's words as recorded in Matthew six.

During World War II there were those who by one means or another were able to get more than their share of rationed goods. It was not uncommon to find pantries stocked with stores of coffee, sugar, and sometimes canned goods, or other items that they thought might be in short supply. Some of these people would brag about such things and would show their friends what great stores they had on hand for emergencies. Their friends of course would usually respond,

"How smart, how clever, how foresighted you are!" It might be that some of these friends would go home wishing that they too had their pantries full of rationed food. Actually they should have felt sorry for, rather than envious of, these others. If one examines the matter casually, he might think that these people were given a feeling of security because of having these extra supplies. Such is not the case. The very fact that they went to all the trouble to get these supplies— and their willingness to use extra-legal methods, proves that they were not basically secure; else they would have gone to no such trouble. These hoarders felt that they could not be happy unless they had ample supplies, and whenever they wanted them, of the kinds of goods that they had been used to. They were admitting by what they did that they were unable, or would be unable, to adjust readily to new situations. Although in a sense it is true that they had feelings of security of a kind because of this extra food, these feelings were overlaid on the basic feeling of fear that in the first place caused them to amass these quantities of food. They were not nearly so well off as their friends who simply bought their sugar, coffee, and other products as their ration coupons allowed. These others were happy to have what they had and not unhappy because they did not have more. These were content with what they had; those who were Christians really believed that the future was secure, even though it might be more sparse than the past had been.

Nowhere in Christian teaching is it indicated that it is good for one to make no effort for himself, expecting God to set the birds to bring food to his mouth. But it is a part of Christian teaching that one should do the best he can; and as a believer in God and the Christian way, he believes that all things will come right. Since it is our feelings that have so much to do with our mental hygiene and thus our happiness, and since the future is always such an unknown quantity, then the person with these feelings has the stable base; this is the person who can face the future unafraid. "And why are you anxious about clothing? Consider the lilies of the field, how they grow; they neither toil nor spin; yet I tell you, even Solomon in all his glory was not arrayed like one of these. But if God so clothes the grass of the field, which today is alive and tomorrow is thrown into the oven, will he not much more clothe you, O men of little faith? Therefore do not be anxious, saying, 'What shall we eat?' or 'What shall we drink?' or 'What shall we wear?' For the Gentiles seek all these things; and your heavenly Father knows that you need them all. But seek first his kingdom and his righteousness, and all these things shall be yours as well. Therefore do not be anxious about tomorrow, for tomorrow will be anxious for itself. Let the day's own trouble be sufficient for the day." This admonition is also from Matthew six.

Many have given such advice, and it has been eagerly accepted by thousands, possibly even millions of people: that we should live from day to day, or in day tight compartments, or just one day at a time. This of course is not an original thought with them. It is most widely accepted as coming from Jesus Christ the Son of God.

It is true that those who put so much store on food and in what feelings of security it might bring them also get more pleasure than may be good for them out of the eating of this food. For all of us who are normal and in good health there is pleasure in eating. God made it thus; otherwise we might not bother to eat. Like so many other of the pleasures of life, food must be carefully controlled and must be a thing of temperance. It becomes disgusting to most of us to see anyone whose sole end and aim in life is eating. Like most things that are bad, this has within itself the seed of its own punishment. Health is lessened, activity is diminished, and physical appearance is not all that can be desired. So we might say that those who put so much dependence on food as a symbol of security and as an emotional expression of security are somewhat drowning their fears—not in drink, but in food. None of this is to be taken as indicating that a person should not enjoy his food. But it is not good for food to become the main thing in life, such that it occupies completely conversation, thoughts, and is the final goal of most efforts. Food is to be used, not to use one.

From ages unsung, clothing has not only been worn for protection but has also been worn as a symbol of various things. That original American, the Indian, although in most cases wearing little or no clothing, nevertheless, had his articles of dress that were symbolic. For some chic and svelte American woman, a mink or a chinchilla wrap may be the evidence of the position that she has reached and the security of its kind that she has found. For early American Indians beads or feathers or other objects such as shells might have a similar meaning to them. So it is not an accident that we have come to use the expression "wear clothing" rather than "use clothing." In the same way many of us wear cars and wear houses. All of these are objects that can be easily seen by our fellowman; and these objects very loudly, although not verbally, say to our fellowmen that we have achieved. And if we can convince them that we have achieved, and in turn we can see that they are convinced, it helps us to convince ourselves that we have achieved; that we have done those things in life that are worthwhile; that we have nearly attained security. But again like the ones with money, if this actually be true, these people should show a calm, serene, peaceful manner in all of their life's corners and turnings. Alas—it is not too often so.

Frequently we find that these people who wear these clothes and these cars and these houses are imperious people; they are difficult to deal with; they are suspicious of their fellowman; they are selfish; and sometimes they have in large degrees many of these other foibles of the flesh that make life difficult in the living of man with man.

"Let not yours be the outward adorning with braiding of hair, decoration of gold, and wearing of robes, but let it be the hidden person of the heart with the imperishable jewel of a gentle and quiet spirit, which in God's sight is very precious. So once the holy women who hoped in God used to adorn themselves and were submissive to their husbands, as Sarah obeyed Abraham, calling him lord. And you are now her children if you do right and let nothing terrify you." These verses are from first Peter three.

In the foregoing passage we have one of the most outstanding thoughts that is woven throughout the New Testament. In other words that which is corruptible and perishable is that which can be seen and is physical. These are the kinds of things that so many people tie their security to. But notice that it is said, "Let it be the hidden person of the heart." The words of the Book indicate that the really valuable thing, the really secure thing, the thing that does endure, is that which cannot be seen and does not depend upon that which can be seen.

The Christian should have an entirely different set of values if he truly believes in Christianity applied, than does the person who is not a Christian. This person does not wear houses; he lives in them. This person does not wear cars; he uses them. This person does not wear clothes just for the sake of wearing clothes, but he wears them because they are utilitarian, functional, useful. It may be that this one is meek and even goes to some trouble to live not too differently from others. For the Christian there is not too much difference in the clothes that he wears from those of others; but certainly there is not such great value attached to them as is attached to them by the people who are not Christians. Thus this person has a great bulwark against difficulties in the area of mental hygiene. This person is not dissatisfied or too discontented if he is not able to have the clothes that he or she would like to have. This person is fairly well content with the clothing that he has, as long as they are reasonably clean and warm and do not make him too conspicuous. They are not even really auxiliaries of his life; they are simply those necessities which must be taken care of briefly and then forgotten. This person does not find that one of the highly competitive areas in life is that of competing with his neighbor or his friends or his associates in the manner of dressing. This person is neither overly excited nor overly depressed by clothing one way or the other; either that of his own, or that of someone else.

Certainly the culture of our modern times is exactly opposed to this Christian outlook. Tremendous stress is placed upon clothes, the way one wears them, the price he pays for them, and the kind of clothes that they might be. In advertising, in stories, in pictures, in television, in radio, and in his own day to day observation the importance of the right kind of clothes is stressed. When we say that this is a part of the contemporary culture, we may do an injustice; because actually as far as can be determined this has been part of the culture of most people of all times. It shows that people are people.

CHAPTER III

Love and Hate

Hardly anyone these days can pick up a magazine or a newspaper without reading somewhere in it about the great need for security in the life of the child. It is true that many of these articles do not go on and explain what this security is, but if one reads with discrimination, he can soon determine what is meant by this security. Summarizing the whole matter briefly, one may say that the small child from birth on needs plenty of love, tender care, physical attention, and enough of the people around about him paying attention to him and taking care of him to prove to him, both with and without words that he is wanted, needed, liked, and accepted. The wasting away of a small child even to the point of physical death may come about through the lack of love and attention. Love, of course, is treated of very fully in the New Testament. The love of God for his children, of Christ for all the world, the love of the husband toward the wife, the wife toward the husband, the love of the parents toward the child, the child toward his parents, the love of a person for his fellowman even including his enemies—all of these are put forth as right ways of life and of living in the New Testament. These were not put here as arbitrary commands, but because God, who is the author of man and his behavior, knows that these things are good for man.

In love is a thing that cannot be seen or felt, yet is the most powerful force that the world has known. All of the threats of physical force that are inherent in millions of hydrogen bombs are not so great as the force of love, a thing which one cannot see; but like electricity, the effects are very powerful.

Possibly there is something that you want someone to do very much. It may be that the person that you want to do this thing is an ordinary human being; in other words, very stubborn, and the more you try to force this person to do this thing, the more he resists and the further away he gets from doing it. But if there is love between the persons involved, and if the doing of this thing is a part of this love, then the thing will be done gladly and willingly and quickly. Thus it is very easy and simple to show that love will move; whereas all the threats of force, all the fear of revenge, will have no effect.

Just as love is a moving force in a positive direction in this way—and unfortunately, a force that the world has never recognized very much nor used very much—so also is the force of love a stabilizing factor in the life of the individual.

There seems to be no shadow of doubt that a person is born with as much need for affection and love, and also as much need to give affection and give love, as one has a need to take in water, air, and food. It is as though this is one of the purposes for which man is made; to love and to be loved. In fact, if we compare our own observation, the results of history, and the teachings of the New Testament, they will all agree that this is true.

We are talking of love in the general sense including all love of all kinds. This love may usually be defined or at least limited to that which helps both or all of the persons involved and is not hurtful to one or more. It is difficult to believe that love moving in a hurtful or destructive way can truly be classified as love.

The Christian is assured that his Father, who is the author of all things and is the giver of all things, truly loves him. Just as the love of parents for the small child is emotionally helpful to the child, it must be that for the adult who believes that he does have a Father who looks after him, and cares for him, and loves him will come a great and wonderful sense of security. Nature may be threatening to this one but God, who is the author and controller of nature, is for him a father of love; and although he may not understand always the ways through which God works, he has confidence that it will be not for his bad or his destruction or his terror or his pain, but will be for his good and his pleasure and his happiness, going on through this life and the life that he believes is to come. Here is something solid to hold to in the midst of depression. Here is something real to build on in the midst of war. Here is something actual and tangible that he can have and that he can grasp even in the days of the greatest threats that the world might throw at him.

This person, as he develops from childhood into adulthood, *if* he has the proper Christian teaching, is taught that he is to love his fellow man. He is taught that other men, regardless of color, or nationality, or education are made in the image of God just as is he. He is taught that these people have inherent within them that which is fine and good and worthwhile. Although he may find it difficult sometimes to understand them and to know what he would like to know about them, he does have faith that these things are so.

As a child he has probably discovered that this love is good for him. He has found that if he shows love towards others they respond in the same way. He has found that love, even in its smallest manifestations, can go a long way and affect many people. Quite often as an adult, when many other things have pressed in upon him, he may lose sight of some of these childish lessons that are so right. Then he is very surprised to learn that sometimes in a difficult situation with one of his neighbors—or it may be some person that he has never seen before—that if he manifests the characteristics of liking and loving the person before him that anger is subdued, wrath is stilled, and that at first one who appeared to have enmity for him, proves instead to want to help him and to do what is good for him.

Thus if he continues to practice this love for his fellow men, never misses an opportunity to do this, and shows his love for his fellow men round about him whether they be good or whether they be bad, he finds that they respond in kind. True, we are not so naive as to believe that singlehanded he will change all the people, their lives, their thoughts, and their actions just by showing love. But what we are saying is a simpler matter; we are saying simply that in interpersonal relationships that when one acts as though he likes others, admires others, loves others, that these others will react in kind. He finds that this great force is a stabilizing force, not only for himself but for the others with whom he is associated.

Sometimes he finds that not always is he man enough or Christian enough to do as he should do. We find that many times he acts as does his fellow man round about him and that he shows displeasure, anger and some of the signs of not loving rather than of loving. And he always finds that he gets a reaction in kind when he does this. But if he is wise, and learns from his own experience, he knows that love does that which force cannot do. Thus he makes this loving a part of his life, and making it a part of his life, his life ever becomes more stable, ever more productive, ever less threatened by others and by the forces that are without.

Love in the New Testament has many faces. Christ said
"You have heard that it was said, 'You shall love your neighbor and hate your enemy.' But I say to you, Love your enemies and pray for those who persecute you, so that you may
be sons of your Father who is in heaven; for he makes his
sun rise on the evil and on the good, and sends rain on the
just and on the unjust. For if you love those who love you,
what reward have you? Do not even the tax collectors do the
same? And if you salute only your brethren, what more are
you doing than others? Do not even the Gentiles do the
same?" This teaching is in Matthew five.

In these words Jesus is binding upon man a mode of
action that is very difficult for him to follow. Man in his
traditional ways of behaving cannot see that such a way is
sensible. Man has always said when one attacks you, attack
him; when one resents you, resent him; when one speaks
spitefully of you, speak spitefully of him. The Christian way
is in direct contradiction to the way of the world concerning
whom one should love. This wisdom concerning human behavior, since it is coming from the One who is the author of
human behavior, is wiser than the wisdom of man. The way
set forth here will work in man's relations to his fellowman;
it is also a way that will make a man's life better for himself
even though the other might not respond to this way.

Love is also indicated as being that which sometimes we
do not regard as love at all. Not many of us think that speaking to a stranger, or to one who is not our friend, constitutes
love. It seems plain that such a simple act is part of the general love that is good for man.

When one walks down the street and meets a grim looking stranger coming toward him, and out of the clear blue
sky he speaks to this grim looking one, there may be a look

of surprise, sometimes a flash of gladness, come to the other's face. This is a simple experiment that anyone can carry on at almost any time from now to the end of the day; one can see for himself that it works.

Because the one who speaks is conscious of the effects it has on others, it cannot help but have an effect upon him as well. He is made to feel better within himself; not only that, but because of doing this to his fellowman, he comes to think more of him. Not that he becomes wiser or more intelligent, but it seems that this one has a broader and better understanding of his fellowman. For one who will speak to friend, enemy, and stranger alike finds it very difficult to have a pessimistic outlook on people and their ways, or to feel that all is bad and no good is left. Such a feeling as this is very definitely a part of good mental health. If all of us felt that the world was in such a state as the front pages of a newspaper depict it as being, we should probably say, "What's the use?"

It is bad for one to feel that he has enemies. Again, may it be pointed out that it is the feeling of having enemies that is so bad for one, rather than actually having enemies, unless, of course, the enemies are actively and aggressively attacking one and hurting him in some way. If one can come to the point of actually loving those who would be his enemies, then he has done well both for himself and for them. If one does not feel that others are his enemies and has learned to love them, then the fact that they might even try to harm him does not bother him too much. It is very likely that he does not even contemplate such a thing.

A common element of our behavior is that we project onto others much of what we are and what we feel ourselves. Therefore if one loves others, and he does not feel that he has enemies, it is unlikely he will be worried about those who actually are his enemies. If he follows the rules of Christian mental health that are laid down in the Bible, he eliminates fear for himself, and he makes it possible for better relations to be established between himself and these would-be enemies; thus he eliminates them as enemies once and for all. There cannot be enmity between two that love each other.

Although it may be true that this love we are speaking of is not the great, moving, emotionally dramatic experience that we so often think of as defining love, nevertheless it is a love that is vitally necessary. In fact we need more of this kind of love than of any other kind of love in the world.

Hate is notoriously bad for one. Many studies have been made of the ill effects of hate upon human bodies. If it were not true that hate also scars the soul and can ruin the life, just what it does to the body is enough. One's blood pressure system may be ruined, one's heart may be made a poorly functioning instrument of the body, one's nervous system may be upset, and finally hate may come to be the ruling force both physically and psychologically in the hating person.

It would be enough to say of love just that it eliminates hate.

And so the Christian who tries to live according to the rules of mental health that are laid down in his Book is one that is going to know more and more about his fellowman, to understand him better and better, and to love him more and more. As he practices these rules of life, he will come more fully to understand exactly why such rules are given. He will not be of the great crowd of the cynics and of the blind who say that such things are impracticable, that they are only ideals, and that they will not work in this tired, tough world in which we live. How the one who loves can come to pity these others who know so little!

It takes very little mental effort for us to see what love would do for the world if it were universally applied. Let us envision for just a moment what would happen if every man loved his neighbor as himself. There would be no stealing— because a man does not steal from himself. There would be no blackening of character, no bearing of false witness— because a man does not do these things about himself. There would be no distrust, suspicion, certainty that one's fellow-man is about to do one wrong, because we do not have such feelings as these concerning ourselves about ourselves. There would be no murders, no cheating, no profiteering, no taking of advantage, no holding of angry grudges that are fanned until they become bitter flames of active hate.

An ideal, impossible, Utopian situation?

Yes, we admit that this is so. But after all the Christian believes in heaven. And heaven is a place like this. The life of a Christian is pictured as being like that life which will be in heaven. Certainly, then, it is consistent for such a system to be ideal. And the strange thing about it, that the world can never understand, is that it is a system that works for those who try it. How foolish can man get, when he looks at the lessons of history of five thousand years, and sees that the customary ways of the world are wrong and do not work? We have intelligence enough regarding mechanical and electrical contrivances that if they do not work, or do not do the job that should be done, to try something else. We have not yet reached the point of reasoning as intelligently concerning our relations with each other. What makes it worse, in that for more than nineteen hundred years now, man has had the way set forth before him clearly, plainly, simply. Truly, the wisdom of man is foolishness with God.

Home, marriage, and the family make up an exacting and a trying situation; and if there is not plenty of love to motivate and to make worthwhile, it naturally follows that such a situation will be unpleasant and hurtful. In the way that father or mother treats the child—in the way that they speak to each other—in the way they conduct their whole lives—if there is not love, it is quickly apparent to the child. It has been said that the first thing that parents owe their children is to love one another.

In the Christian system of mental health, such an outstanding thought is not overlooked.

"Husbands, love your wives, as Christ loved the church and gave himself up for her, that he might sanctify her, having cleansed her by the washing of water with the word, that the church might be presented before him in splendor, without spot or wrinkle or any such thing, that she might be holy and without blemish. Even so husbands should love their wives as their own bodies. He who loves his wife loves himself. For no man ever hates his own flesh, but nourishes and cherishes it, as Christ does the church, because we are members of his body. 'For this reason a man shall leave his father and mother and be joined to his wife, and the two shall become one.' This is a great mystery, and I take it to mean Christ and the church; however, let each one of you love his wife as himself, and let the wife see that she respects her husband."

"Now concerning the matters about which you wrote. It is well for a man not to touch a woman. But because of the temptation to immorality, each man should have his own wife and each woman her own husband. The husband should give to his wife her conjugal rights, and likewise the wife to her husband. For the wife does not rule over her own body, but the husband does; likewise the husband does not rule over his own body, but the wife does. Do not refuse one another except perhaps by agreement for a season, that you may devote yourselves to prayer but then come together again, lest Satin tempt you through lack of self-control."

Here in Ephesians five and first Corinthians seven, we find teaching in a few simple sentences that if the world would but heed, the world would be a better place. It is intended in Christian marriage that each love the other as much as he loves himself. If at the start of marriage the two people concerned recognize this, they are going to set this as one of the ends, aims, and goals of marriage. They will not be too concerned with satisfying only their own wants, needs, and desires. They will be just as concerned in satisfying the wants, needs, and desires of the other one involved. The Christian teaching in this relation is not saying that one should be *entirely* concerned with the other. It does say that one should not be selfish, and that he or she should think just as much of and do just as much for the other as he does for and thinks of himself.

This of course does not happen over night. It is something that comes only with long practice, with strict attention to this thesis as being good, and working at it. And in such a marriage, when children come to it, they will find an atmosphere that brings security in every particle of it. Here is the greatest gift that a mother and father can give their child or children—real, true, growing love for each other. Much of it will rub off on the child.

Such a matter of the flesh as sexual expression is taken into consideration in Christian teaching. It is shown in its true light, not only as passion, or of the flesh only—but is shown that the fullest sex expression has its place in the scheme of real, developing love of a man for a woman, and a woman for a man, in marriage.

In the foregoing selections from the New Testament it is shown that each should think of the other in the area of sexual satisfaction just as much as he thinks of himself or herself. It is shown that each can understand the other, and the needs and desires of the other, and that they should see that the mutual needs and desires are met. It is also shown that a purpose of meeting of these sexual needs is for the coming of children into the family relationship. It is good for mental health for children to be in the family; this is one of the reasons that God in his plan and in the Christian way gives his sanction to the family.

Certainly in the normal, average home, no one can deny the good effects of children. Here two can see in a concrete way the truth that they are one flesh. Here is a human being— a personality wherein one can see and discover parts of the other. This makes for more closeness, and this makes for greater love.

And love, which is a part of God, makes for better mental health.

Love is the greatest enemy of mental illness.

CHAPTER IV

Fear

The obverse of fear, security, has already been treated at some length in this book. Since fear is probably a constitutional part of the natural man and works for both good and bad, as do so many of our emotions, it is in order that we give more than just a passing discussion to it.

Christian teaching is full of references concerning fear; how through the resurrection of Jesus Christ man can come to conquer his fear of the unknowable and non-understandable enemy death, and the lesser fears of almost as incomprehensible life.

Fear within us is not an accident.

If there were no fear of fire, we should be continually getting burned. If there were no fear of bodily injury, we should forever be getting run over by cars and trucks. If there were no fear of shocks, we should constantly continue to be electrocuted in our own homes. God put within each of us this capacity for fear that we might more or less automatically respond to threatening situations and not spend all of our mental energies telling ourselves: "Be careful now, that will burn you. Cross the street only when the light is with you, or you'll get run over. Don't grab those two bare wires, or you'll wish you hadn't."

It is true that in the beginnings of our fears of these things we were subjected to a combination of verbal teaching concerning these dangers, plus some experience with them and their unpleasant results. Almost all of us have been burned or shocked, if not run over by an automobile. So once this fear is instituted, we behave in such a manner that injury is prevented, without doing much intellectualizing about the matter.

These are the kinds of fears that do not hurt us in any way, if they are normal, and we want to see them, to a degree, instilled in our children and all the other human beings about us. If any of these normal fears develop into phobias, then of course they are bad for us. Usually they do not.

Many volumes could be written about man's fears through the ages. How many things man has feared, and fears: the unknown, disaster, gods and gremlins and devils, witches, disease, famine and drought, flood and hurricane, the dark, animals and Indians, thunder and lightning, the far reaches of the ocean and the towering heights of mountains. And it cannot be denied that his very fear has been the motivation to cause man to be the conqueror of many of these; but as he conquers one fear, he invents a new one. H bombs, A bombs, or C bombs; the earth is dying, or else is coming closer to the sun all the time; a new ism springs up, more virulent than the last; we are in imminent danger of being invaded by indescribable creatures from a neighboring planet; Russia is going to beat us in getting an artificial satellite to circling the earth; and it is rumored that already the atomic explosions on the earth have spread a layer of radioactive poison in the stratosphere that will gradually filter down and destroy all life on the earth. In the meantime, according to this rumor, this atomic energy has already upset nature's balance and all the freak weather we are having is because of this, and really, we haven't seen anything yet compared to what is to come.

We make fun of our ancestors of generations gone who had such unreasonable fears. Yet we, in the spotlight of twentieth century knowledge, may behave even worse than they.

Science, knowledge, progress have done nothing to allay fears, largely because man is what he is and has always been, and partly because science, so-called, is only what man makes it. Scientists are men with the same foibles, prejudices, fears, hopes, and weaknesses as other men, even though the popular idea may be otherwise.

For instance, look at virus x.

Two generations ago no one worried about virus x, because no one had ever heard of it. A child was sick; people either knew what was the matter with him, or they did not. Today a child is sick. They either know what is the matter with him, or they do not. But if they do not, many times the physician will say, "He has a virus."

Now polio, the common cold, influenza, and various other diseases have been so well publicized that nearly everyone knows they are classified as virus diseases. Saying that one has a virus may engender more fear than saying, "He's sick, but I don't know yet what is the matter with him."

Could it be that as science lays one fear, it raises two more? What the proportion is, we could not say. But we can say that increasing knowledge of physical things does not allay fears. An increasing knowledge of God's creation and His relationship to it through His Son will help to allay fears, however. This is the perfect way; all other ways work only in part. This way works wholly and completely.

Not too many years ago the declaration for the New Freedoms was announced by the heads of two of the greatest governments on earth. One of these was the declaration of

Freedom from Fear. But fear has increased, not decreased, since then; and once again man has learned that governments, power, and money cannot insure against fear. Freedom from fear must come from some other source.

In the annals of history to come, it may well be that this age will come to be known as the Age of Fear.

As present evidence of this, following is an Associated Press dispatch, datelined St. Louis;—"Parental fears of atomic warfare are contributing to the 'nation's number one problem'—Juvenile delinquency—Dr. Daniel L. Seckinger, public health director for the District of Columbia said today.

"While he declared there are many other contributing factors—including maladjusted homes, substandard health, welfare and recreational conditions in certain areas, and lack of proper job opportunities for teen-agers—Dr. Seckinger told the 48th annual meeting of the Southern Medical Association:

" 'The atomic blasts, aggression overseas, the threat of war, the (military) draft, the facility of mobility, and other factors have tended to accentuate our national problem No. 1.

" 'With the development of the atom and hydrogen bombs we have become the first generation in history which, we can realistically say, is living under the threat of total annihilation.

" 'This threat is reflected in the anxieties and uncertainties of parents who in turn impart them to their children.' "

What Dr. Seckinger did not say, and it probably has much more bearing on the question than most of what he did say, is that present day teenagers have been brought up in a social milieu that fosters delinquency. In a world—the only world that they have known—where nations, including our own, promote their world wide aims largely through the threat of violence and death, where shadows and repercussions of this violence eddy and flow through our domestic relations, both economic and political, where only material means and goals and achievements are set up as offering security—delinquency must be part of the fruits of unstable homes in such a community setting.

If anti-social acts are acceptable on a world-wide basis, it is not too hard to see that the young, who are sometimes more intelligent than the old, will logically adapt variations of such acts to suit their own life patterns.

And where does fear enter into this latter part of the picture, one might ask?

What is a nation, actually? Groups of people—individuals—who call themselves nations, and act accordingly. And if people live by groups, and are afraid of the people in the other groups, we have the situation existing that now exists. Since we usually attempt to destroy our fears, the most direct attack is to destroy the thing or person that causes our fear. If we fear that we will not have enough things, we increase our efforts, honestly or dishonestly, to get those things. If we fear that we will be classed as inferior by others, and we believe that we can remove that stigma by getting something— power, or fame, or money or reputation—that is identified with us, we attempt to do so by this means or that. If we fear that we will lose the race, or the game, or the fight, we attempt to allay those fears by cutting corners and by cheating, or by playing dirty, or by hitting below the belt. If great groups of people approve such practices, and shout in unison: "The end justifies the means!" a lone voice or two crying out against such carries little weight.

It is the truth, then, to say that the present day teen-ager lives in an age and a time that fosters delinquency, for he lives in an age and a time of fear, with its unhappy results.

Does a good and a stable home, rooted and grounded in trust and security, based on Christianity, make any headway against such times and practices?

The answer is unequivocally yes.

The Christian home is a home of faith, not a home of fear. Here the parents, the first representation of the world to the child, feel secure and impart this feeling of security to their children. They live in a world that has no more bad things in it than the world has always had, and the Creator of this world is their Father Who is not unmindful of them and Who will see that they are not hurt more than is good for them. The future holds no terror for them through atomic death or any other tremendous catastrophe, for their Father loves them, as proved by the sending of His Son and as told in Romans eight.

"Who shall separate us from the love of Christ? Shall tribulation, or distress, or persecution, or famine, or naked-ness, or peril, or sword? As it is written, 'For thy sake we are being killed all the day long; we are regarded as sheep to be slaughtered.' No, in all these things we are more than con-querors through him who loved us. For I am sure that neither death, nor life, nor angels, nor principalities, nor things pres-ent, nor things to come, nor powers, nor height, nor depth, nor anything else in all creation, will be able to separate us from the love of God in Christ Jesus our Lord."

Then for the child that is born and reared in a home like this, there will be no fear of total annihilation, nor fear of what the future will bring, because the parents of such a child are secure and serene, and this security and serenity are imparted to the child.

Death is no tragedy, only a victory, for the Christian; so he does not fear death in whatever form it might come. Life is the real battle, but in this battle neither can he lose, for he still is walking with the touch of the hand of God upon him, and he is not removed from His love. There is no power, nor combination of powers, that can overturn him nor undermine him, for God is his helper and his stay. And if God through His words can create the universe, His child need have no fear of what might happen to him, understanding only that whatever might happen, of pain or of pleasure, will work for his good. He is more than conqueror through Him that loved him.

In a stability of life and home such as can be under these circumstances, it will indeed be the exception rather than the rule to find a child who becomes a delinquent.

Comic books are blamed by some adults who are cognizant of the sad facts of delinquency, and who must blame something besides themselves for a social order that fosters delinquency. But children whose lives are built of the solid material furnished by a Christian home may contact but will not be hurt by such things. Other adults place the blame on the picture shows, the radio, the television, literature, the public schools, the lack of religious emphasis—anywhere except where the blame squarely belongs—on their own muddled shoulders.

The young will feed upon the food furnished by the old until they can forage for themselves. By then their appetites will be fixed. This food comes from the total environmental diet, not from a dab of seasoning here and there.

One of the great sources of fear for the human being comes not from the natural man, but from the cultivated man.

There is nothing "natural" about being afraid that our position in life will suffer because of others. This is a completely cultivated thing. In most psychology texts it is spoken of as a part of the socialization process. We are taught that it is good to learn to get along with people and to like people; these are part of the plus side of the socialization process. Very little is said of the minus side.

This minus side consists of being afraid of people, not of what they will do to one physically but of what they will think, say, and do in relation to the one who has the fear. This is learned, and all can readily see that some of this fear of others is necessary for a well balanced life. The man or woman who has only contempt for other's reactions to one's own self does not get along well in life. And so it is for the man or woman, boy or girl, who is always afraid of the reactions of others.

One of the most prevalent fears of our modern American adolescent and adult is the fear that another, or others, are above them in some particular respect. This we usually speak of as the feeling of inferiority, or the inferiority complex. It consists largely of fear, and this fear is entirely learned. There is no shadow of evidence to show that fear like this might be inborn to any extent.

This fear is quite generally based on our materialistic and non-Christian outlook concerning achievement and success as measured by the average man. The Christian outlook is quite different, and exceedingly better. In Matthew eighteen the matter of greatness, stature in the eyes of men, relative position and success became foci of concern for the disciples.

"At that time the disciples came to Jesus, saying, 'Who is the greatest in the kingdom of heaven?' And calling to him a child, he puts him in the midst of them, and said, 'Truly, I say to you, unless you turn and become like children, you will never enter the kingdom of heaven. Whoever humbles himself like this child, he is the greatest in the kingdom of heaven.' "

Christ was not teaching humility as a measure of greatness by accident, or as an escape or defense mechanism, but because being the Son of God and a co-author of man, He knew what works for man.

An extension of this teaching is found in Matthew twenty when the mother of the sons of Zebedee, believing success to be what the world for long has said it is, asked that the worth of her two sons be recognized and that they be given a high status on the right and left hands of their Lord when He came into His own. Her request did not gain the coveted places for her sons, but it did bring down the indignation of the other disciples on the shoulders of the two sons. They immediately sensed that if such a request were granted, they would feel inferior because they too had not attained such an eminent position. So they were made afraid, were made to feel inferior, and immediately struck out against the potential threats to their own self-esteem. In this particular case the actions of all of the twelve, and the mother of two, followed the pattern that the world has so long taught.

But Christ said otherwise.

He said in Matthew twenty that "Whoever would be first among you must be your slave."

Serving is not the world's idea of success. From time immemorial, the servant has been only a little higher than the slave, and the slave has been only a little higher than the dog. Yet here is this strange Man of Galilee teaching that greatness lies in serving; that success is not found in plaudits, acclaim, or notoriety, but in service. Surely this is the most radical teaching that the world has ever known!

But in such a teaching, we find a double bitted axe of worth. It works to the good of the one serving, and the one served. It is an aggressive and a positive teaching of *goodness*.

In seeking greatness through service, one is not made afraid of the ones that he serves, because he is not competing with them; he is not trying to wrest from them anything that they might have; he is not trying to supplant them in any position or place of favor. He is only trying to help them; only trying to supplement what they are already and what they have already. Consequently he cannot be afraid of them, for there is no basis for fear. Likewise the ones being served are not afraid of the one serving them, for they recognize in him the lack of threat to anything that they might be or are. Their reactions to the one serving them may not be Christian, but at least they are not fearful, and thus they are much more likely to treat kindly this person seeking to serve them. The exception is the person of so-called position who treats shabbily those serving him, because he is so insecure, afraid, and unsure that the only small measure of status that he can achieve within himself is to see himself, feel himself, and hear himself treating others in such a manner. This person then is to be pitied, for a present hell burns within him even though he may be envied by thousands for the worldly eminence that he has attained.

The one who seeks greatness through service is not ridden by fear of the results or of the future. He is not afraid of rebuffs, for he knows that they will come and are to be accepted just as he accepts sunshine and rain in their proper portions. He is not afraid of lack of appreciation for his efforts because he knows that the worth of what he does lies not in appreciation and words of praise, pleasing though they are, but that the good lies just in the serving.

This is strong meat and only for the grown-up in emotions and intelligence. The immature find Christianity a very difficult Way of Life. Most of us are disgusted and discouraged when we try to achieve some small measure of greatness through service, as we look around and see how little others value our efforts. It is then that we may decide to give up what seems to be the hard way and the unspectacular way, and to go back to the way approved by most—use any and everybody for a stepping stone to the top, while ridden with fear every minute of the way that one misstep, one slip, and we too will become only a stepping stone to the top that we did not reach. In our blindness and ignorance we fail to see that there is no top; and if there were, and it could be attained, that it would have no contentment or peace or joy attached to it. In our blindness and ignorance we do not see that the one who goes serenely on his way, seeking little but to justify his life by being of service to others, is walking a path of tranquillity and satisfaction with no one to shove him off or block his way; that there is a path for everyone who wants to walk this way, and that the paths are all parallel. Two may stretch out their hands from path to path to support each other, but never do they put out their fists.

As we study the abnormal emotional reactions of the people round about us, we find that the people who are in worst shape are people who are always undergoing catastrophic situations. Although to us the event or circumstances or situation may seem fairly normal, to these disturbed ones it is always a catastrophe.

Herein fear is able to work with its deadliest poison.

Read about a paranoid who became psychotic through fear. This is a composite case-history.

James C. Charles was a young man. He was a person of good intellect, and had a vocabulary that was the envy of many people who were normal in every respect. In fact he could talk so convincingly—and in most areas so seemingly rationally—that the ordinary person might suspect him of being a mad genius rather than just plain mad.

But if one talked to James long enough, his paranoia would begin to emerge; James was so afraid of death that he had evolved the delusionary system that through power of thought one might ward off the ravages of age and thus live forever.

While talking to James on most subjects, he would talk vigorously without too great an excitement. But when he began to steer the conversation into his favorite channel, as he nearly always did, he would become flushed, tense, and would sometimes work himself into such a state—especially if the one he was talking with opposed him in any way—that he would get rigid in posture, his breathing would come rapidly and shallowly, his eyes would nearly close, and he would show physical symptoms of an extreme agitation.

In a long series of talks with James, he brought out many of the things that had contributed to his illness.

He was a child of the depression and was brought up in a home that found the financial way very difficult during the formative years of his life. He lived in an atmosphere of fear which subtly filtered into every crevice of his being. His parents likely did not recognize that their fears were absorbed by the child then multiplied and intensified a thousandfold; but they were.

James was the only boy, and as a result was more carefully looked after than was good for him; and many of the restrictions that were placed upon him were restrictions that were touched with fear. "Don't do that, you'll get hurt. Don't let your clothes get so messy, or no one will like you. You can't have that, it might injure you." And so on.

Certainly it is not being implied in relating the above portions of James' life that there should be no restrictions on a child. There most definitely should be.

But if most of one's life is made up of restrictions, and these restrictions are based on fear, then each one simply teaches the child to be more afraid.

So James grew up becoming more and more afraid. He found a job as an adolescent, performed his duties well, and kept the job for quite some time. But throughout the time he worked there was little or no enjoyment of the job, and it was merely a means to an end—a way to run a little faster from the fear that always pursued. In his school work he excelled, afraid to take things easy in the light of the urgency that was life. In his main recreational outlet there was the pressure to excel in performance, the fear of not doing well enough.

And along the line as James grew up, he absorbed many fears of many things in many ways. Little by little these churning and rolling fears of his life began to spiral, and at the vacuum of the center they began to circle around one fear that could embody them all. The fear of death.

Because of many contributory reasons, James' formal religious training did not imbue him with a weapon against the fear of death; but he did borrow in a distorted way the fact that believing and practicing Christianity makes one conqueror over death—but his own persistent and all consuming idea came to be that one could conquer death simply by never dying; that immortality could be achieved while mortal.

James' own thinking that led to this, and James' own reasons for coming to such a conclusion certainly followed a logical although by no means a reasonable pattern.

James thus had to come to believe, because of his intense fears, that he was afraid of nothing. When, in conversation, he was told that he was fundamentally afraid, he denied it vehemently, although in the course of the same conversation he made the statement that no one would ever know how afraid he had been.

So because of his great fears, and the fact that every day was a new and threatening catastrophe in a fearful world, James, to live, had to defend himself in some way. Along with his delusional system that he was learning how to live forever, he also believed that he was never wrong and could not be wrong, and that no one else alive could equal him in righteous living. These things being so, and he wanted them to be so within himself so very much, then there was no cause to fear. And if he could ever come to believe them completely, then all his fears would disappear.

Christianity takes a man away from madness, not toward it.

True, mankind in the past nineteen hundred years has so distorted Christianity that sometimes his version of this religion has worked for bad and not for good. This was not Christianity, however, and all who take the time to find out for themselves what Christianity is know that it brings peace, not disturbance—contentment, not dissatisfaction. So today, if a man or woman in his madness shows signs of projecting his religion into it—and one always projects one's life into his madness—some professional men who do not always know as much as they should, say, "Their religion has made them mad."

This is impossible if the religion is true and simple Christianity. If people believe in a God that cares for them as ? a person, knowing their every need and want before they themselves recognize it—if they believe in God's Son who has known all the suffering of man that He might be more sympathetic and merciful and longsuffering—if they believe that all the power of both God and His Son are ready to work for them for their good; if, believing all these things and believing that the unknown of death will become the knowable through their religion and believing that eternity will be a multiplication never ending of all the best that time has to offer, how can one such believer have anything ever but the soundest mind and the most stable emotions?

Among those common fears that sap us of happiness and energy and productivity are the fears that are attached to envy, jealousy, and covetousness.

This is not to say that these emotions are made up only of fear, but it is to say that fear is a part of all of them—sometimes a great part. It is easy to ascertain that in envy we want what another might have in the way of position or honor, that in jealousy we want the time or attention of another, and that in covetousness we very strongly desire something that we do not have—and in all of these, we are afraid that we are not what we ought to be if we do not obtain our desires. Since fear is such a strong medicine, carrying us to the brink, and sometimes over, of madness, as fear works in these emotions they become more and more threats to our mental health.

It probably goes without question that every adult has more than once in his or her life experienced one, two, or all three of these emotions. Usually this is only a fleeting experience, and no indelible imprint is left on one because of his experiencing; but there are those whose lives are ruled and ruined by these poisonous emotions.

In the Christian Way there is a simple rule that really works in the lives of those that follow it—a way that works to eliminate envy, jealousy, and covetousness. Christ gave the teaching in His sermon on the mount when He said: "Blessed are the meek, for they shall inherit the earth."

Here again the teachings and traditions of men have fouled up the minds of human beings to such an extent that they have difficulty in accepting such powerful teachings. The world believes that meekness is synonymous with cowardice, but the meekness that Christ is talking about is the very antithesis and antagonist of fear.

The meek are the ones who can say, "All is well."

The fearful cannot say this and never say this as long as they are fearful. In fact this is what fear is: the feeling that all is not well, that something must be done at once.

One common dictionary definition of meek is "mild of temper; patient under injuries; long suffering."

So the meek is not injured when someone he loves pays attention to someone else; he is not injured when a friend has more than he has, for he knows that the material is really immaterial; he does not ardently desire with all of his fleshly fibers to have something that has no real connection with happiness. He knows that these world-taught ways are specious and misleading.

He is not injured because he has no pre-set fears that if he shares attention and time, if he has less than others, then he is somehow inferior. He sees that personality is worth more than personableness, and that the material trappings of life are but stage settings, never sufficient to make up for a poor performance.

Not only is he not injured, but he is made positively happy with what comes his way, for his life is a positive one.

This one who has learned the good way of meekness is also one who is loving and loved. And even the most cynical philosopher has to agree that love casts out fear; although he may not believe in the divine inspiration of the book that says this.

We do not fear that which we truly love. Unfortunately there are so many ways in which people fool themselves into believing that they love, that some will at first deny this. But real love, that meets the test of time, has no fear in it.

The meek one is glad when those he loves have attentions and favors from others; for he does not fear these attentions and favors, knowing they cannot undermine his sure and secure relationships. And since he truly loves, it is as though these attentions and favors and sharing of time were not only the loved one's, but are his, for he loves this other as himself. So where there is love, and true Christian meekness, there is no fear and will not be jealousy.

This is not to say that never will there be any twinges of sharp but impermanent feelings of jealousy; for we are still human beings and have absorbed the teachings of the world round about us, even though we may not accept them. But it is to say that these will be only momentary disturbances and will not by any means be a rule or a basis for life.

When good things come to another, whether they are material things or otherwise, the meek one who is truly the fearless one is made glad and happy. Such events do not hurt him nor put him in an inferior position and do not set new standards that he must somehow meet, while fearing that he will not. Since he has learned to love and has learned not to fear, he is not touched with envy, because it cannot penetrate the shield of love and fearlessness and meekness.

The covetous want more not because they have too little, but because they are afraid, in comparison with those round about, that they do not have enough. If they should be completely isolated from other human beings, and had what they needed to keep them alive, warm, and busy, it is incomprehensible that they should desire a finer car, or home, or clothes, or position, or salary.

Thus the practicing Christian is as far removed from fear as one can be on this earth. He believes the statement in Hebrews thirteen that "the Lord is my helper, I will not be afraid; what can man do to me?" He believes with the Sweet Singer of long ago as given in Psalms twenty seven, "The Lord is my light and my salvation; whom shall I fear? the Lord is the stronghold of my life; of whom shall I be afraid?"

These questions in their simplicity carry the logic of their incontrovertible answers.

These who believe and practice such things walk unafraid through life. They are not afraid that when two whisper behind their backs that it is necessarily something bad about them. They are not afraid that a stranger they meet on a dark street will be able to harm them very much. They are not afraid that every sales clerk will make a stupid mistake that will cost them, and they are not afraid that each person they do business with is dishonest and will cheat them.

They do not have to pick on the smaller, the weaker, and the less fortunate than they to prove how secure and fearless and strong they are. The virtues of security and fearlessness are within them, a part of their heart and a part of their mind, and they do not feel compelled at all to prove to others that they are this way.

How pitiful is man wallowing in the pits of fear, when at his own choice he can ride on clouds of glory! If man but looks to his Elder Brother, believing not only that He is the Son of Man but also that he is the Son of God, he will know that he need have no fear, and that what he seeks, he will find, and that what he asks, this will be given.

He may not miss trials nor suffering nor tribulation; neither will he miss happiness and serenity and peace. But he will miss fear.

He will miss the fear of death, of war, of radiological disease and disaster, of poverty, of depression, of disease, or accident, of domestic catastrophes, of the ill will of mankind. He will miss all of these—and how wonderful is their missing.

CHAPTER V

Conditioning

It is not often that we can experiment with dogs or cats or rats and apply the results to the behavior of the human being—although too much of this is being done today.

One experiment, done many years ago on a dog, did produce some results that indicated the generalization involved would also apply to human beings, and later work has proved this to be true. This experiment came to be known as the original conditioned response experiment. Its implications, applied to all forms of life that are capable of learning, are tremendous.

The experiment came about like this—a physiologist named Pavlov was experimenting with the hunger drive and consequent reactions in a dog. It was readily observed that whenever food was brought near the hungry dog he would begin to drool in preparation for the pleasant time to come. Pavlov had a bell sounded each time that the food was presented to the hungry dog. It was noted after this was done a number of times, that by simply sounding the bell, with no food in sight, the dog would start drooling and would give all the pleasant anticipatory reactions that he normally gave when the food was presented. This is conditioning.

However it was also noted that if the bell were rung at intervals, with no food being presented, soon the dog would stop drooling and would show only the normal signs of reaction to the sound of the bell, such as opening his eyes, pricking up his ears, or looking around.

What causes such reactions?

Possibly the simplest explanation is that the organism is never responding only to one stimulating force at one time but always is responding to a variety of stimulating forces. Thus the dog came to respond simultaneously to the presentation of food and the ringing of the bell, and quickly the separate responses of drooling and listening attentively became so completely interlinked that soon the stimulation of either the bell or the food would cause the drooling. But for such activity to continue, the pattern of reactions has to be reinforced; that is, at intervals the food would have to be presented with the sound of the bell if the drooling is to continue at the sound only.

One of the strange things about conditioning is that many times the stimulating situation may be replaced by a substitute. By this we mean that in place of the bell, a bell-like sound may work just as well to produce the reaction—the tinkle of ice in a glass, or the clinking of two metallic objects. It is this ease of spread of the stimulating force that makes conditioning even more potent to reckon with in human life.

The same experiment has been tried with human infants and works just as well, although in a somewhat different manner. Most infants will flex and draw up their leg when tickled on the bottom of the foot. One infant was repeatedly tickled on the bottom of his foot at the same time that a buzzer was sounded. After a while, the buzzer alone was sounded, and the infant responded exactly as though his foot were being tickled.

It is a common occurrence amongst older people to find those who do not like orange juice. As children they were given orange juice mixed with castor oil—when they needed medicine—on the theory that the orange juice would make the castor oil more palatable. What their parents did not foresee was that some of the children would forevermore respond to the stimulation of orange juice as though it were castor oil, and would actually find that the orange juice later on *tasted* like castor oil.

In conditioning, we find one of the keys to much of our behavior and the kind of mental health that we enjoy, or fail to enjoy.

Long ago we learned that a certain situation, such as the authority of an over-severe parent, brought unpleasantness and pain. Soon we learned to feel unpleasant and painful even before the situation had completely developed. But after a while we passed on from the sphere of influence of this parent into another sphere of authority. But if we were conditioned strongly enough by the feeling that authority gave us in the parent-child relationship, we may have all or part of those same feelings of pain and unpleasantness in relation to any kind of authority—teacher, officers, court, military, neighbor, or whatever. When this happens, we are in for a bad time.

But conditioning works just as well in a pleasant direction as it does in an unpleasant direction.

Here is a family with two children—a small girl who has a brother two years older than herself. All of her childhood this growing girl is treated kindly, considerately, helpfully by her older brother. The majority of their relationships are of the most pleasant. Through him she develops a feeling, or response, for all boys and men. As she goes on through life, because of her conditioning, she sees in every man and boy a little of her older brother, and has a little of that same warm feeling toward them that her brother's treatment of her engendered.

The working aspects of Christianity depend greatly on conditioning.

Christianity is a teaching religion, and conditioning is a learning process.

Today our world is in bad shape because we have given mostly lip service to those things that work for our good and have had too little conditioning in these same good things.

We are told that God is love.

But for this to become a part of our lives, we have to be conditioned to it. What child, growing up in a home where petty revenge, enmities, and slow burning hatreds are the rule of life can come to know more than just the sound of the words "God is love?"

How many people we know that cannot wait to avenge each little slight they might receive, are always feeling that their neighbors or business associates are out to "get them" if they can, are always nursing some ill feeling for some one! If these people are parents, they can take their children to church seven times weekly, with not too much hope that the child will ever rise above his conditioning.

And in how many homes do parents make such remarks before their children as they read their papers: "Well, I sure hope they hang him, and hanging is too good for him. . . . Those dirty so-and-sos in Slobbovia; why we oughta take a couple hydrogen bombs and wipe 'em out! . . . Well looka here, haw! haw! haw! didja see where ol' Giltrix is bein' sued for a million dollars; I hope they get every cent he has!" Possibly the parents do not put such attitudes into words; but if they have such attitudes, you can be sure that the children absorb them, and are being conditioned thereby.

It is true that the human being is able to rise, because of other educational processes, above his conditioning. Many times our early conditioning is not continued, and we forget the common responses, and learn a new set of responses later on in relation to new and better conditioning.

Such a process is technically called reconditioning, and is usually slower than the original conditioning; since something has to be unlearned as well as something new learned.

Some boy or girl may grow up in a home where they are conditioned to feel that marriage and conjugal relationships are made up only of fussing, fighting, fuming, and feuding. Later as they get away from home, they may have the happy experience of being reconditioned, and finding that there are happy marriages, and that some husbands and wives love each other deeply. The reconditioning may come about through their own marriage; by the power of their own intellect they may reasonably avoid some of the pitfalls that their parents fell into. And with each new success in this great adventure of life, they find out how infinitely more satisfying such a condition is than one of continuous strife, and thus their new conditioning may become even stronger than their old conditioning was. Their early conditioning will be a powerful influence; it may cause them to defer marriage, or to put it off altogether, or to make some mistakes in their own marriage. But it is not an insurmountable barrier, especially if they are willing to use their reasoning powers, and if they understand such basic principles as conditioning and how it works on them.

Animal training is simple conditioning.

How pitiful it is to see many children of otherwise intelligent parents that are not so well trained as a puppy.

Because of the asinine ideas of some psychologists, pyschiatrists, and pediatricians of the thirties that a child should not be inhibited, but should be allowed to grow up his own little (heathenish) way, some parents even today, in spite of the teaching of today's psychology, still do not believe in "training" their children.

Simple conditioning in the training of children operates as follows: a crawler or toddler has the opportunity to explore his first hot stove and be burned. As he reaches for it, mamma says "No." Probably little toddler has not yet learned what no means; so the hand goes on its exploratory way. As the hand comes close to the stove, and toddler feels the heat therefrom, and mother at the same time sharply slaps little toddler's hand as she says No—and the hand should be slapped hard enough to hurt toddler—the little one immediately gets the idea. Being an independent little individual, as most toddlers are, he may experiment another time or two in order to see just what it is about the stove that is forbidden. But if each time mother sharply slaps his hand, and shows plainly her displeasure, the child is then conditioned to understand that reaching for the stove is dangerous and fraught with painful consequences, and being an independent little individual with a lot of intelligence, he has learned—has been trained—to leave hot stoves alone.

From this conditioning process there are a number of parallel effects that we should discuss.

The child, in this simple training process, learns the true meaning of No. This if applied sparingly will be just as effective in other situations where No is in order. No has now come to mean for the child that he had better take it easy, or parental displeasure and physical pain both will be the resultant.

For the No to continue to remain effective it must be used sparingly, only in the cases where necessary, and may have to be reinforced occasionally. If the parent says No too often it loses its power, because many of the times when No is said and not enforced, the child re-learns that No isn't attached to unpleasant consequences. So it must be used only as needful; and if the meaning of No diminishes, another time or two of hard hand-slapping connected with it, while mother's firmness is quite apparent in her voice and manner, and the child will again be conditioned to the meaning of No.

In like manner and possibly even more powerful is the conditioning force of reward. This may be praise or satisfaction on the part of the parent, obviously shown to the child in connection with some activity. Probably the reward should not often be anything tangible, for then the child may be conditioned to respond in the parentally approved way with the thing he is to receive always in mind.

Although pleasant relationships, praise, mutual satisfaction are rewarding and are sufficient for conditioning, love should never be used as a pawn to gain one's way with a child. If this is done, it almost automatically guarantees that such a love will become ineffective; that it will offer no reward to the giver or the receiver. Worse, love used in such a way engenders ill feeling and even hatred; a small child is intelligent enough to realize that such love is no love at all, and to become increasingly resentful that he has no security in a simple love, freely given.

For conditioning really to work both pleasantness and unpleasantness must enter into the picture. The child must know, if he is to live with people, that there are certain things

that are unpleasant. He should understand that the pleasantness and unpleasantness are practically automatic; that they
are parts of a simple cause and effect relationship. All of
this is true in the conditioning process, and the conditioning
process is the secret of most training—whether of children
or puppies.

In Hebrews twelve there is the most direct statement of
New Testament teaching regarding this matter. "My son,
do not regard lightly the discipline of the Lord, nor lose cour-
age when you are punished by him. For the Lord disciplines
him whom he loves, and chastises every son whom he receives.

"It is for discipline that you have to endure. God is treating you as sons; for what son is there whom his father does
not discipline? If you are left without discipline, in which all
have participated, then you are illegitimate children and not
sons. Besides this, we have had earthly fathers to discipline
us and we respected them. Shall we not much more be subject
to the Father of spirits and live? For they discipline us for a
short time at their pleasure, but he disciplines us for our
good, that we may share his holiness. For the moment all
discipline seems painful rather than pleasant; later it yields
the peaceful fruit of righteousness to those who have been
trained by it."

The whole basis of this book is that God who made man
is the supreme authority concerning what is best for man.
So when God speaks through the New Testament concerning
the way man should and should not behave, no psychologist
nor psychiatrist nor philosopher anywhere can gainsay Him.

And He says that a father, or parent, that loves his
children will train them—discipline them—even punish them
if it is for their good. Present day psychology—blessings on
it—agrees. And this training, this disciplining, is a part of
the conditioning process.

Punishment that is properly a part of the conditioning process is never vengeance or the venting of wrath or retaliation. To be effective it must operate in a framework of love. To be effective it must always relate cause to effect, and the child who is being conditioned through punishment must realize the cause-effect relationship. And punishment to be effective must be moderate, yet severe enough to be decidedly unpleasant, not continuous, and for one purpose only—to help condition the child in the right modes of behavior that will bring him emotional stability through his entire life.

If we are wise enough to recognize such facts when our children are young, and are even wiser in that we can recognize when to act and when to relax, then proper conditioning through the span of years of the child when conditioning is most effective will practically guarantee that our children will never be problem children. Solomon knew what he was talking about when he commented that if a *child* is trained up in the way he should go, when he becomes old he will not depart from this way.

There are many evidences to indicate the real need of discipline in the life of the average person.

The small child is a helpless creature and must depend on its parents or other adults completely for the satisfaction of its wants. This is as God planned it. But if well meaning though ignorant parents, or too busy parents, or indifferent parents, or cruel parents allow the small child to go its own way with no conditioning, then the child is wandering aimlessly in a world that it cannot understand, solve, or cope with. And without exception this child becomes a nervous wreck— or if you prefer to be a little more technical, becomes neurotic.

As a case history, there was one child adopted into a home when the parents were approaching middle age. Understanding little of the needs, dynamics, and behavior of a child, they thought it was the part of love to give the child every thing that its little heart desired, and to deny it nothing. In doing this way they so disturbed the child who was living in a world without rules and a world that was artificially centered around the child that the child became moody, had terrific temper tantrums, was allergic to an entirely too long list of things, and evidenced all the symptoms of extreme neurosis, if these same symptoms had been present in an adult.

This child needed the parents to treat it not as a live doll but as a child with needs and desires not only to be met, but also to be denied. And if these meetings and denials are set up rationally and sensibly and administered in this way, with plenty of opportunity for the child to learn and explore independently; then immediately the child's world will fall into pattern, because then its world will become a world of rule, order, and means and ends, centered not too much but enough on the child.

Lest someone misinterpret all this, let it be said that the other extreme made up of complete domination and authoritarianism is just as bad as giving the child no conscious conditioning, for conditioning of one kind or another is always there. Completely dominating and controlling the child's life will result in as bad psychological and emotional end products as letting the child stumble blindly around. No parent has the right to use his child as the scapegoat of his own emotional shortcomings. Just because the act of dominating may make us feel superior is no excuse for dominating our children to the point that their emotional health may be impaired or ruined.

An outstanding case study of the power of conditioning came to light when a twenty year old college man came one day for help.

"I'm afraid I'm in real trouble," was his opening statement.

"Why?"

"Well, I don't know whether you know it or not, but I'm a preacher's son. You would think that someone like me would get more pleasure out of going to church than almost anyone else, wouldn't you? But I not only do not get pleasure out of going to church—I hate to go."

"Yes?"

"Yes, I do. Now I don't think there is anything really wrong with my faith—I think I believe in God and Christ just as strongly as anybody, but I have to force myself to go to church. I don't miss going often; I go nearly every time I am supposed to; but I just hate to go."

"There must be a reason."

"Yes, there is; and I think I know what it is, after we have been discussing conditioning in class. Back when us kids were small, daddy was very sensitive about our behavior in church. If we so much as whispered or wiggled and he saw it, he'd punish us for it after church. Any number of times mother would get up during his sermon and take me out and spank me if she thought I was misbehaving and that daddy would see it. So it seems pretty obvious to me now that church was made a pretty unpleasant place for me when I was little, and without knowing it, that feeling about church became so strong that it stays with me even now."

This young man was a better self-analyst than most, for it seems that his reasoning was correct.

"I think I agree," the counselor answered. "What you have just said is a well known fact but calls forth very little thought. The strongest memories that we have are feelings or emotions. A favorite flavor may be such because it had such a strong and pleasant impact on us as children. Childhood is a time of feeling and not of thinking. Childhood is the time when we are conditioned to love home or hate home; to love school or hate school; to love church or hate church. These feelings, once attached, are very difficult to root out."

The young man looked thoughtful. "Right now, I want to know what I can do about it. I want to keep on going to church; but I want to enjoy it, not feel the way I do about it now."

Here was launched a discussion of reconditioning. Now that the young man knew the source of his feeling about church was a fairly natural thing, and not a decay of his faith, he had taken the first long step in outwitting his emotions. Understanding that now he could approach church attendance from an entirely new emotional viewpoint, and that time itself would be on his side in helping to eliminate the old emotion of unpleasantness connected with church and to substitute the new, reconditioned emotion of pleasantness and satisfaction, he left the conference declaring that already he felt that he would enjoy church the next time he went more than he had ever enjoyed going before.

In a simple life situation such as this young man had undergone, we can find some clues to human behavior that some psychologists and psychiatrists—especially those with no religious outlook or foundation—have long interpreted mistakenly. Some of these say that religion itself is sometimes interpreted as the cause of the trouble.

This appears nearly always a mistake.

But what is true is that emotional experiences stemming from what people sometimes *call* religion do actually affect some persons adversely, and a reflection of their feelings in this area is always apparent.

The faith, hope, and love that are the context of Christian living never did and never will have an adverse effect upon a human being; if faith, hope, and love become a part of one's life, this person is taken farther and farther from any likelihood of neurotic or psychotic behavior. These basic elements of Christian living make one secure, give one a feeling of contentment, peace, and joy, give one a purpose for living and the ability to conquer death. These fibers of the Christian cloth are strong and everlasting, elastic enough to fit every troubled soul. They hold together—they do not cause disintegration. They cement the personality into something that is good to behold; they do not undercut it from within.

But if in place of the elements of true Christianity are substituted harshness, cruelty, self-righteousness, and unmercifulness—and if a man or group of men and women are quite vocal in their binding such things on people in place of Christianity—then every psychologist, psychiatrist, and Christian would agree that such things could make one mad, and such things might be found as a strong reflection in the feelings and words of madness.

In summation concerning the relationship of conditioning, Christianity, and mental health, we can say this: emotions connected with life experiences are strong, very strong, especially if these are childhood experiences. This emotional tone or coloring that is connected with a situation or experience can easily flow to other parts of the experience or situation, and cause the whole situation to take on the feeling of a part of it. To illustrate simply again, a child may come to hate school because of the ineptness, harshness, and emotional balance of one teacher. This feeling of dislike for the school situation may stay with him as long as he lives and color not only his actions, but his attitudes and thinking.

So if a person is to come to believe in and practice Christian living, he must be conditioned to it. If as a growing and developing personality he is conditioned to respond to Christianity in its specific and general aspects with feelings of pleasantness and satisfaction, this personality will integrate into its thread and fiber Christian principles and practices and will in turn be reinforced in this conditioning because of the satisfaction that the practice of Christianity will bring.

But if this developing personality is conditioned to a pseudo-Christianity that brings an emotional state of unpleasantness, dread, and fear, then he will likely avoid completely not only that which passes for Christianity and which has formerly conditioned him in the wrong way, but he may also avoid real Christianity until he can be reconditioned.

In the reconditioning process words only will not suffice, although without doubt they will help. There must be those around him who not only say, "I believe in Christ as the Son of God"; there must be those who prove that they believe in Christ as the Son of God by their actions. There must be those around him who, by their actions toward him and his own emotional response, show that they love him as themselves, and that it is not a matter of lip service only. There must be those around him who practice forgiveness, meekness, humility, fearlessness, hope and practice these things in such a way that this developing personality gets the full emotional impact of such parts of the perfect way of life. Thus his conditioning, or reconditioning, will progress in the right direction.

Conditioning is one of the basic ways by which a personality learns.

And as Christianity is a teaching religion—as Christianity is a way of life that prevents rather than foments madness, pain, fear, and insecurity—as Christianity is a way of life that foments rather than prevents joy, peace, contentment, happiness, hope, and faith—we must not overlook the great part that conditioning plays in the development of a Christian life.

CHAPTER VI

Frustration and Aggression

Probably there are no inborn instincts in the human being at all in the same sense that insects and animals have instincts.

An instinct is an inborn pattern of behavior; the honey-bee can make a perfect honeycomb without ever seeing it done; the digger wasp can sting a caterpillar in exactly the right place to anaesthetize him without any previous instruction or a course in Digger Wasp Anesthesia.

In the human being there are no such patterns of instinctive behavior which limit the performance and function of the insect. He is capable of modifying his actions continually through teaching and learning. God made man this way, distinct and separate from the rest of life.

The tiny infant manifests a sucking response when he is hungry and he can get anything in his mouth; he sneezes when his nose is tickled; and he blinks his eyes if an object approaches too close to them. These are properly classified as reflexes, not instincts, since they are generalized responses. All of these reflexes can be modified through conditioning and other forms of learning.

What about the instinct of self-preservation? This is not a true instinct, either, as a brief examination will readily show.

Every day you read about a human being that takes his own life. You will never find proof of a lower animal doing this, although some imaginative writer now and then may assert that such is so. And history is full of thousands of cases of men and women who have allowed death to come to them without seeking to save themselves if they feel their life is being given for a cause. Others have deliberately taken their own lives, not in the cold light of reason, of course, but nevertheless contrary to all the mechanisms of the supposedly strong "instinct of self-preservation".

As one example of these generalized reactions that human beings possess, any one will struggle and attempt to set himself free if he is suddenly caught from behind and held tightly, and most especially if a hand is placed over his nose and mouth so that breathing is restricted. This reaction is common to every conscious human being, infant, child, or adult. This is much like the reflexive reactions of sucking, sneezing, or blinking.

If we are caught from behind and held tightly, and our breathing is restricted, we are frustrated. If we have been going along normally pursuing our goal of unrestricted moving and breathing, and suddenly we are blocked in this pursuit, we manifest all the signs of anger, with possibly some fear, and because of these emotions—feelings of aggression— we increase our efforts to get back to normal, again to achieve the goal of unrestricted moving and breathing.

It is universally accepted as a fact that when frustration comes, aggression usually follows. This aggression may be directed toward an object, person, or self, or may be a combination in any proportion of all of these. Thus some who are frustrated explode, some seem to fold up, some seem to try harder, some seem to roll up into an emotionally impenetrable ball. There may be as many manifestations of aggression as there are individual personalities.

One of the worst manifestations of aggression is in the form of long continued wrathfulness that is directed towards a person and persons and burns hotter with the passing of hours and days. This kind of aggression almost invariably results in destructive action and it is even more destructive to the personality of the one that harbors such feelings. It is this wrath that is the father of hate, and we have already briefly treated of the physical effects of hate.

It is this kind of aggression that is so deplored in Christian teaching and is pointed out as being so wrong because of what it does for us and others.

Christ said in the sermon on the mount as recorded in Matthew five, "But I say to you that every one who is angry with his brother shall be liable to judgment; whoever insults his brother shall be liable to the council, and whoever says 'You fool' (or graceless wretch), shall be liable to the hell of fire."

Herein we can trace the growth of anger into wrath that impels the possessor to words and action, and many times the end result is, if not murder, at least the desire to murder. Here we find Christian teaching dealing with aggression in its worst form.

Such feelings of aggression arise from some frustrating circumstance in relation to another. And the ways are legion in which others can frustrate us.

Only rarely do they actually interpose themselves between us and the goal we are pursuing, except in the case of small children and parents. But in other ways they can just as surely and certainly block us. Many of these ways are fairly obvious; the policeman blocks the street we are traveling and makes us turn right when we wanted to go straight on; the teacher tells us we are mistaken when we know that we are not. A neighbor or friend or acquaintance achieves more or acquires more in some particular area than we do and makes us feel that we are failures, and sometimes not liking to blame ourselves and accept ourselves as we are, we at least partly blame him and feel aggressive toward him.

More often we feel aggressive toward some one because he injures our ego, and without a doubt the ego is the most tender part of the individual. It is well to remember that ego is the main part of egotism. A person says something to us or about us that is injurious to our self esteem; this is blocking or frustrating to the continuous expansion of self esteem; so normally we feel aggressive. We may not growl and snarl to show our feelings of aggression; instead we may carefully control any showing of feeling. But this is no indication that the feeling is not there. It usually is and too many of us harbor the feeling and remember the words, turning both over and over as we roast them above the glowing coals of bitterness and baste them with the gravy of self pity and feelings of inferiority.

As we feed such feelings of aggression, the whole incident may begin to assume such a position of importance as to become the all consuming passion of our life. This will not happen, of course, to the well balanced individual, for he will soon forget and thus automatically forgive.

For the emotionally maladjusted, he will carry the thing on and on within him until somehow, some way, he has to save face, get revenge, and put the frustrator in his proper place—which may be a grave.

Are we then never to feel angry at all? Are we, as we seek to live the Way of life, never to feel frustrated or aggressive?

Possibly opinions should be left completely aside and we should let the New Testament answer.

"Be angry but do not sin; do not let the sun go down on your anger, and give no opportunity to the devil." This admonition of the Book is found in Ephesians four, and the meaning seems to be rather clear.

The sin of anger is not in the fact that anger wells up within us but in what we let anger do to us. We may not always be able to control this artesian spurt in every circumstance, but we can prevent our feeding upon it, dwelling upon it, taking it to bed with us at night, getting up with it in the morning.

Herein is the sin (and sin is always harmful to ourselves, or others, or both) of anger—that it be nurtured. This is not to indicate that anything we do in the white heat of sudden anger is all right, because no such teaching nor inference is given in the New Testament. We must always be accountable for our actions as long as we are sane.

It seems very plainly taught that there is no wrong in the simple feeling of anger; it is where we go from there that counts.

The good Lord that made us did not make us to be forever spinning our wheels in anger, or to be helpless in the grip of any other emotion, with nothing to be done about it.

So He instituted in us the process of sublimation which seems to work especially well for us regarding aggression and our sexual urges.

Sublimation, if we interpret it in the idiom of the times, means "out of this world". In chemistry we talk about solids that can be sublimated; these solids if heated will go into the gaseous or "higher form" without becoming liquids first. Thus the material becomes "sublime", or of a higher order than its original state.

Raw aggression may be a rather ugly thing resulting in barbaric action, and the sex urge in some circumstances becomes lust and bestiality. Both aggression and the sex urge are powerful forces, *but with the ready possibility in the human of being channelled into a higher order of activity rather than just exploding into uncontrolled expression.*

So let us assume that when we are frustrated, whether we show it or not, we are also made to feel aggressive. Let us assume that it is a fact, and most psychologists say it is, that this aggressiveness must be worked off in some way if we are to remain emotionally healthful.

We can work it off by a direct physical attack against the frustrating object or person. We can work it off by an attack that is more indirect, such as an attack with words. We can work it off by an attack on something entirely apart from the frustrating object or person; for instance, if the boss frustrates us, we may later take the aggression it arouses within us out on the dog, or the wife, or the children. Usually it is the dog or the children; this is less dangerous.

Or we can work it off by an attack on a task or a situation that may be entirely unconnected with the frustrating objects or person, and we may in this attack accomplish that which is socially and personally advancing and satisfying. This is sublimation.

The Christian Way forbids the direct attack upon the person frustrating us. But if you will examine Christian teaching concerning such situations, you will find that the

Christian is told to control his emotions (of aggression) through intelligence, and then *to do something about it*. Look at the latter part of Romans twelve.

"Bless those who persecute you; bless and do not curse them. Rejoice with those who rejoice, weep with those who weep. Live in harmony with one another; do not be haughty, but associate with the lowly; never be conceited. Repay no one evil for evil, but take thought for what is noble in the sight of all. If possible, so far as it depends upon you, live peaceably with all. Beloved, never avenge yourselves, but leave it to the wrath of God; for it is written, 'Vengeance is mine, I will repay, says the Lord.' No, 'if your enemy is hungry, feed him; if he is thirsty, give him drink; for by so doing you will heap burning coals upon his head.' Do not be overcome by evil, but overcome evil with good."

The golden text of this passage is "Do not be overcome by evil, but overcome evil with good." Here is the teaching to use our heads in using our emotions. If the emotion of aggression rules uncontested, we do that which will hurt first ourselves, then others. But if we think, even though we feel the strong tides of aggression flowing within us, we take this energy and re-direct it into a constructive channel. And what could be more effective than taking the energy that aggression arouses within us, controlling and directing it with our intelligence, and using this very same energy to accomplish good for the one that harmed us? In the process we completely defeat this enemy, this doer of evil, for he cannot be an enemy long with those that treat him like a friend. All of this calls for action of some sort—and of a rather drastic sort—and it is action that helps sublimate our aggression.

Many of us have learned this for ourselves in other ways.

Here is a man who gets tremendously angry with his wife whom he loves very much—except right then. His feelings of aggression are so strong that he feels he has to attack her in some way, and in our present day culture it is usually with words. This in turn causes her to feel aggressive, and believing that a good offense is the best defense, she attacks in turn. Such a circumstance can be fraught with grave peril.

But if instead of working all of his aggression off in a wordy attack with all its attached dangers, the man is wise enough to plunge vigorously into the activity of the moment— repairing a leaky faucet, mowing the lawn, unsticking a balky door, writing a report, studying for the next test in the correspondence course he is taking—if the man is wise enough to use up most of this energy that goes with aggressiveness in constructive effort, he will be no end surprised to find that soon he is feeling normal again, that he loves his wife as much as ever, that the world has reassumed its everyday color and proportions, and that life is good after all. Such a way of handling aggression is in no whit theoretical; it has been proved workable in thousands, possibly millions, of cases.

So the process of sublimation, then, is simply using the energy aroused within us for constructive rather than destructive purposes. We as Christians are not commanded never to feel aggressive; we are taught to learn to use this aggressiveness in a way that works for the good of all.

It is utterly unrealistic to think that husbands and wives, employers and employees, neighbors and nations will not ever frustrate each other and thus bring about aggressiveness. But it is realistic to understand that unless much of our aggressiveness is sublimated our world will revert again to the law of tooth and claw, if A bombs and H bombs and C bombs can be considered in such archaic terms.

Is there not some way to handle this aggressiveness before it gets started? Do we have to wait until we are frustrated and aggressive, and be forced always to be looking for some way to sublimate this aggressiveness?

The answer is yes to the first question, but it is a more difficult way.

The answer lies in the causes of frustration which we have discussed briefly, and in the reasons why some of us are frustrated more easily than others.

Much of our frustration is brought about by the world in which we live. Whether our own frustrations of our present age are greater or less than those of another age no one knows for sure. It is the opinion of some that man's frustrations, as to quantity, change little through the ages but only arise from different sources.

Today we have made such scientific and technological advances that soil, air, and water cannot frustrate us long; we are their conquerors as God intended for man to be. But as we are frustrated less by these things, we are frustrated more by the artificial goals and barriers that we have created.

Our children go to school to learn; but both we, their parents, and their teachers, all too often think they go to school to make grades. Consequently the child that makes A's is a success, the child that makes B's is just so-so, and the child that makes C's is, relatively speaking, very mediocre. And it may be that the child who makes B's is more frustrated and has more a sense of failure than the one who makes C's. In high school the child who makes A's may be frustrated as much or more than any of them; a boy may feel distinctly cheated because he was not physically endowed with the equipment to make the football team. A girl may feel that life has tricked her because her complexion is not so smooth, her features so regular, or her hair so beautiful as the girl who is featured throughout the school yearbook.

As these children leave the life of the schoolroom for the life of home and job, they face a new series of frustrations. If they do not have as nice a home, do not drive as fine a car, do not make as much salary, do not advance as rapidly as William or Joseph, they may feel they are failures; life has let them down; and they may live with a constant sense of frustration.

All of these things are artificial, and there is not one really frustrating thing about them, other than as we have been taught that they are frustrating. And although we may be taught that a situation is frustrating, it may be as frustrating as if it were an uncrossable river or an unclimbable mountain.

Actually the child who makes C's in school, if that is his level of ability, is just as much of a success as the child who makes A's. The family who lives in a very modest home is just as successful as the woman who can afford the most modern in kitchen equipment and who serves the best of frozen and precooked foods. The man and wife who earn and barely live on a few hundred dollars a month are just as much of a success as the man and wife who earn and scarcely manage on five hundred dollars a month. But too many of them in every bracket feel more frustrated, thus aggressive, than they ought, for they live too much by artificial standards that have been set up through the ages on a basis of appearance, and not on the real basis of what is good for the individual.

Is there Christian teaching that will help us in this particular area?

Most assuredly.

Christ said in the sermon on the mount, "Blessed are the meek for they shall inherit the earth." And the Holy Spirit further voices the same thought in Hebrews thirteen, "Be content with what you have; for He has said, 'I will never fail you nor forsake you.' "

Even though in this book we have already discussed the meek and their inheritance of the earth, it is fitting that we discuss this matter also in relation to frustration.

Often people get the mistaken impression that meekness is softness, vacillation, lack of opinion, fear of others' opinions, a gelid and spineless reaction to the challenges of life, even cowardice. Nothing could be further from the truth. Christ, the perfect example of meekness, never evinced the slightest indication of any of the above.

Meekness is the spirit of acceptance; the understanding that much of what life brings is unchangeable; that we can change what is changeable and readily accept the rest, good, bad, and indifferent.

Herein then the meek do inherit the earth. If one has developed this great Christian quality to the extent that what life has to offer him is good—that finally it will all work for his good—this one truly has all things. And he has all things without the frustrations, frettings, and fumings that his non-meek brother has, who in turn gets at most only a very few of the things that he wants of life, and these things have to be tangible and countable.

So the one who learns meekness by the very same process learns to be less frustrated than others. He has found a new way to achieve the things that are good in life, and there are few frustrations in the path of his achieving these things. Since he does not have to possess these things, call them his own, be able to touch, taste, handle them, and put them into barns and banks, he will not be frustrated in relation to them. But those who do have to touch them, taste them, handle them, and put them into barns and banks find a never ceasing array of frustrations before them as they chop, hammer, butt, and gouge their way to getting more and more and more. How strange it is that the world calls a man a success who has chopped, hammered, butted, and gouged more out of life than his brother!

The road to less frustration is by learning acceptance of those things that are unchangeable, by learning that the standards of the world are not the standards of the happy human heart. With less frustration there is less aggression; with less aggression, there is more energy for love and for right relations among men.

Thus for the meek there will be a minimum of frustrations; he is not often frustrated in his relations with his fellow man, for his fellow man is more often not a competitor but a helper. He is not often frustrated in his goals and ambitions, for the Lord is on his side, and he cannot fail—even though the Lord in His own wisdom may change his goals and ambitions for him. He is not often frustrated in his desires for material things, for they are only a means to an end, after all, and not the ends of life. They are the shadows, not the substance.

This is the Christian way, and the mentally healthful way, to defeat many of life's frustrations before they happen; to be more acceptant, more easily adjusting to the changing pattern of life. To be able to ride with the blows, to be able to take advantage of the currents going in the same direction, to be optimistic opportunists. In none of the teachings of Christianity is left the thought that one is to react to life with Oriental passivity, sans feeling, sans effort. Instead he reacts to life with vigor and force, sure that God knows the way better than does he, and willing to accept His will in a spirit of meekness, doing what he can, leaving the rest to God.

Frustrations for such a one will be few and feeble.

CHAPTER VII

The Unbending Neurotic

The most prevalent kind of emotional disturbance is neuroticism.

Usually we do not think of the neurotics as being mentally ill, for they are not hospitalized in the sense that they are committed to some kind of institution, public or private, for treatment. Nevertheless they are ill; they are so off balance emotionally that their life is seriously disturbed, and usually so are the lives of all of those with whom they have intimate contact.

Already in the beginning of this book the subject of neuroticism has been rather summarily treated. Now we want to consider the matter both at greater length and in relation to Christian teaching and Christian living.

Basically the neurotic is an insecure person; if Christianity takes enough on one, he does not feel insecure except momentarily, thus cannot be classified as a neurotic. We have already agreed, you see, that all of us that have become adult do at one time or another exhibit occasional neurotic behavior patterns; but this is far from making neurotics out of us.

The neurotic is a neurotic because he constantly faces life with the same framework of attitudes and feelings. Since insecurity is the basic condition of neuroticism, it is only natural that the neurotic strives hard for security. In fact he overstrives, if there be such a word, and it is this overstriving that causes him to act and react as he does.

This chapter is labeled The Unbending Neurotic because for one who is insecure, new patterns of behavior, new ideas, new channels of action, new and unknown vistas over the horizon are disturbing if not frightening. Not that new sights and new sounds are frightening, for the neurotic may be a great traveler; but new situations that call for a new pattern of behavior are definitely unpleasant.

There is a reason for all this.

When we first come into the world, the majority of us come into a rather secure world made up of eating, sleeping, being loved, being changed, being made comfortable, with all of this done in a rather uniform manner, and sometimes quite on schedule and at regular intervals. So this first world that we know that has a nice, warm, loving mamma and daddy always near the center of it is a good world, a secure world. Later on we face the possibility of some rather shocking experiences when we have to learn that for a part of every day we must leave this secure world for one that is not quite so secure and has less love and much more ferality in it. If in the first few years of our development we have been taught in this framework of love and security how to adjust to a world that is not so loving and not so secure, we shall probably never be neurotic. But if the security of life is maintained too long as an *outside* thing rather than as a feature inside of us, we may forever be attempting to revert to those patterns of behavior that formerly gave us a feeling of security, whenever the situation calls for an entirely new pattern of behavior.

Paul said, "When I became a man, I gave up childish ways".

The neurotic is forever reverting to childish behavior in an attempt to find that feeling of security that he may have once had but is now so elusive. There are a multitude of these patterns: complete dependence upon another person—chronic illness, for a sick child is always an object of attention and seeming affection, with all its cares being met—a constant demand to be mothered or fathered, even when forty—fearfulness to take responsibility—seeing the world always with oneself as the center—and on and on until the list of patterns seems almost endless.

This need to feel secure is one of the greatest needs of the infant and small child; if this need is denied, there is much evidence to indicate that forever this person as youth, adolescent, or adult will be seeking to find his emotional security. If he seeks it in the wrong way as he often does, he is sure to be in trouble.

Here is the girl who came up in a home, or without a home, unwanted, unloved, insecure. This is the girl that so often when sexual maturity has been reached, believes that sex activity brings love, affection, and security. She is only too keenly aware that it does not bring happiness.

Here is the boy, coming up under similar circumstances, that persists in antisocial behavior to the point of delinquency. This behavior at least brings him attention, usually some status of a kind.

Probably much more often such a lack of security early in life simply motivates the persons who suffer the lack to demand of those adults they are nearest to that this security be furnished them now. And as so often is the case, they go about it in the wrong way, for one does not receive security on demand. They may bully, dominate, wheedle, play on sympathy, throw jealous tantrums, become clinging vines—and even though such behavior gradually worsens the total situation, they continue unbendingly in such behavior. The causes and symptoms of neuroticism are breathtakingly numerous.

Most if not all neurotics are basically self-centered. A little thoughtful examination shows such a statement to be practically a truism.

The neurotic is in the grip of the unpleasant and painful because these feelings interfere with his ordinary, usual activities. Although a few people can deliver a day's work in spite of very intense feelings, if these feelings go on and on they will invariably take their toll; for these feelings long continued thus become a part of one's personality, and whatever work we do, or whatever action we perform is a product of personality.

The neurotic is in the grip of unpleasant and painful feelings, with himself as the center. "*I* can't do what he can do. . . . That makes *me* sick. . . . She's prettier than *I* am. . . . I don't have as much as *I* deserve. . . . *I'll* show them. Why does all this have to happen to *me*? *I* feel so inferior. . . . *My* health is so poor. . . . *I* am a failure. . . . *I* am so incompetent. *My* luck is always rotten. . . . Everybody is against *me*. . . . Nobody likes *me*. . . . Of all people, *I* am most miserable!"

As the counselor sits and listens to the neurotic he hears over and over again these statements either directly or implied. And these attitudes or feelings, are a fixed part of the personality of the neurotic. Most of his mental capacity, most of his feeling capacity is turned inward and onto himself. One psychological viewpoint is that such a person does not like himself, and this is probably true. It is obvious to every

skilled observer, however, that such a one is more concerned
about himself than he is about anything else. Every feeling
is magnified and intensified; and since so many more of his
feelings are unpleasant than pleasant, the net output of unpleasant feeling is very high.

The neurotic suffers more than anybody else; physical
pain hurts him more, grief is more intense, suspense is more
unbearable, work is more enervating, injustice is more unjust,
the callousness of the average human being is more brutal,
and life is more hopeless to the neurotic than to others. It
could not be any other way, of course, with the neurotic the
great center of things.

So the neurotic attempts to adjust by going too far; he
is always an extremist. Not only is he always an extremist, but
in attempting to adjust he follows the same procedures that
have not worked previously, and usually makes his plight
worse. He may demand all of the attention of those round
about him, or he may pull back into his own shell, telling himself that he cannot be hurt by anything that is said or done.
He may be a buzz-saw of energy, ripping into life eighteen
hours a day and sleeping only fitfully the other six, or he
may be a sluggish ne'er-do-well that sleeps eighteen hours a
day and rips into life only fitfully the other six. He is never
offended, he is always insulted; he is never hurt, but is always
killed; he does not just feel bad, he wishes that he could die.
Other people are not just thoughtless, they are cruel; life
does not have two sides, it has only one side and that side is
a black side. He may either be always attacking too aggressively or running away too fast. The neurotic's mind may be
brilliant, sharp, incisive; but in the areas where he most needs
to use his mind, he uses his feelings. And since his feelings
are persistent and fixed, he uses his feelings in the same way
every time.

What relation is there between neuroticism and Christianity?

Christianity is a way of life. Neuroticism is a way of life. The two do not exist together.

The force of Christianity is inherent in the facts that it is a way that is learned and that man is a teachable being. As mentioned before man has no clear cut instincts but is limited only by what he can learn.

Neurotisicm is a learned way of life. Christianity is a learned way of life. If one learns the Christian pattern of outlook, attitudes, thoughts, and actions then the neurotic way is precluded.

This is not to say or infer that the neurotic has considered and chosen between Christianity and neuroticism, and has favored neuroticism. No human being by choice would choose to be neurotic, for it is a painful, unpleasant, unhappy state of being.

The neurotic is usually the product of neurotic forces exerted by parents, family, and social environment over a period of many years. These first ones to surround the neurotic have taught by example and by responses this young one to be neurotic. It would likely be impossible to find a human being who for years has been a well-adjusted normal personality who in a period of a few days or weeks becomes an out and out neurotic. True, a well-adjusted adult may, because of completely different circumstances during the latter part of his life, change to a semi-neurotic. But this is very unlikely, for without doubt the human being gravitates much more toward that which is pleasant than toward that which is painful; and these ways that have worked early in life to bring good are not easily discarded. Experimental evidence indicates that such ways are as tenacious as ways which bring discomfort and pain.

To promote a clearer understanding of some of these ideas, let us look at a composite case history of a number of neurotics (all of them living people) and treat their combination of characteristics as though belonging to one neurotic. Let us call this composite character P. N. Richards.

P. N. Richards is a young male adult somewhere between thirty and thirty five years of age. He is married and has two children.

P. N. shows a variety of neurotic symptoms in his everyday life. He hardly ever hits an even emotional balance but overdoes all of his emotions. When he gets angry with his wife or children, he is little short of violent. When he makes amends for his emotional binge, he goes on another and becomes almost cloying in his efforts to right the situation.

He feels very insecure in his relations to others including his wife and children. In his attempts to compensate for his feelings of insecurity, he over-reacts, and sometimes feels, and even acts wildly aggressive. If this aggressiveness takes an overt form, it is most likely to be against those who are nearest to him, and who are least likely to retaliate.

P. N., vaguely recognizing much of this, makes his own situation worse by despising himself. He is made to despise himself even more because in trying to make himself feel more secure, he has set goals for himself that are probably unrealistic and unattainable; and if not achieved, then he is a failure, and did not his parents and his society teach him that a failure is a disgrace to be despised?

Vaguely recognizing his own ugly feelings in relation to those he loves and those who love him, he feels that in between times he should give them everything, worry about them, and fret over them. These feelings, of course, are not pleasant, and there may creep in, without P. N.'s knowing it, a feeling of being caught and trapped by those he loves, and even a feeling of very strong resentment towards them, which brings on stronger feelings of remorse because he has the feelings of resentment.

If all this vortex of feeling becomes more than P.N. can handle, and he cannot continue to function in anything like a normal manner, he may begin to exhibit varied symptoms of his neuroticism. He may develop fears of objects, things, or situations that are symbolic of his general state of fear. He may be obsessed with recurring ideas, or feel compelled to repeat certain actions. These also may be symbolic and may also represent a sort of security for P.N. because of their constancy. And P.N., now much more a creature of feeling than of reason, continues to travel in the same vicious circle.

What happened to bring P.N. to such a state?

The basic cause was that P.N. came up in a family that was saturated with fear. So fear as a generalized thing, became a fixed part of P.N.'s attitudes and outlook.

The family of P.N.'s was afraid of everything; most especially were they afraid that they would not make enough, would not be able to pay their bills, would not be able to get by the next summer, would not be able to save up enough for their old age.

They were afraid of disease, contamination, accident, injury. Much of the conversation that P.N. had from his parents was: "No, don't do that; that's dangerous; that will hurt you; you might get killed; be careful." P.N. may not have learned to be afraid of ghosts, goblins, or ghouls, but P.N. certainly learned to be afraid.

The fearful person is not secure, and P.N.'s insecurity was naturally centered within himself. So as P.N. progressed through life, having a good mind, much of what he learned, absorbed, and accomplished was useful to him only in so far as it helped him to compensate for his fears.

If he could be a great man—if he accomplished some fine thing that would make the whole world talk—if he could get rich—if he could achieve power—then everyone, including himself, would recognize that he was not the pitiful, torn, fear-ridden creature that he was.

So P.N., as long as his feelings continue to rule his life, will be a neurotic.

It is fairly obvious to determine wherein P.N.'s upbringing departed from the Christian way. Christianity, *if truly believed and practiced,* casts out fear. Christianity is a life of love with the statement even being made that God is Love; and perfect love casts out fear.

What child, in a good, stable home that is based on love, fears? There is nothing to fear, because mom and dad are ever present helps in time of need. They took care of yesterday, didn't they? Day before yesterday is too far back to remember. They are taking care of today, aren't they? Tomorrow is so far away that it is even hard to imagine.

So then the adult, if he is following his Father, and looks to Him for help that he cannot furnish himself, will not fear. From Psalms fifty five, Luke twelve, Phillipians four, and first Peter five we find a few of the hundreds of statements having a bearing on this topic.

"Cast your burden on the Lord, and he will sustain you; he will never permit the righteous to be moved. . . . And he said to his disciples, 'Therefore I tell you, do not be anxious about your life, what you shall eat, nor about your body, what you shall put on. For life is more than food, and the body more than clothing.' . . . Have no anxiety about anything, but in everything by prayer and supplication with thanksgiving let your requests be made known to God. . . . Cast all your anxieties on him, for he cares about you."

For such beliefs to become an ingrained part of one's life, influencing it away from fear, they must be lived daily. It does not suffice to say the words as a catechism; it does not suffice to repeat the words over in Bible classes, nor to listen repeatedly to them falling from the lips of the preacher, unless one believes them and does them.

And the doing has to start today, and continue for every day.

This is very difficult for the adult who has been brought up to fear. But it can be done and has been done by people unnumbered.

The adult, because of his own experiences, can recognize that much of what he has feared in the past has never happened. He can bring his intelligence to bear on the matter and recognize that energy spent in fear will make him less able rather than more able to meet an emergency. By his own reason he can see that he lives now, this minute; that the mistakes of the past can be nullified, and even be useful to guide one's present steps, but that no man can take a mortgage on the future. These are steps away from fear but rarely can a neurotic take them alone.

He is too fixed in his vicious circle; he is too intent on his own feelings; he is too absorbed by his own feelings of inadequacy and insecurity.

But if he can bring another human being into the picture to help him break the chain of his reactions, to help him grasp a viewpoint that is outside himself, to help him re-view and re-evaluate his own motives, feelings, and actions, to help him most of all to understand why he is what he is and to recognize that through his own powers of learning that he can effect a change—if, we say, he can or will do these things, a happier and more effective life can soon become a reality.

Neurotics do not have to stay neurotic.

Not if they take advantage of all the help that both God and man hold out to them.

CHAPTER VIII

Within and Without

As we consider the matter of mental health, there are a few fundamentals that are simple but important.

One of the most important of these fundamentals is that the way an individual feels about any circumstance, situation, or person is the thing that matters.

A corollary of this is that one's actions in any circumstance or situation or toward a person will be an outgrowth of the way he feels. "As a man thinks in his heart, so is he." This includes a man's mental and emotional activity, and no truer statement was ever made.

If we were to state these fundamental theorems another way, we might say: "A man acts like himself."

As we progress through life, we come to have rather definite ideas about self, and our life revolves around this center. What we tell ourselves in words about ourselves may be quite different from what we really think about ourselves in the innermost core of our beings. The professional psychologist speaks of such a differentiation as being the conscious and unconscious. All of us recognize that our final springs of action come from this innermost idea although we may consciously put up a "front" to hide this truth from others and from ourselves as long as possible.

This has been dramatically illustrated in some episodes of sleep walking and sleep talking. In such activity it is accepted as a fact that the "unconscious man" takes over. Here the desires, fears, and wishes that make up a large part of that innermost self can take over without our conscious or wakeful mind interfering.

John K. was a young man who was an outstanding scholar during his junior year in college. He worked hard, made almost a straight A average, and was very pleasant to talk to and be with; although every now and then he would show a very intensely serious streak. He also worked part time as an instructor's assistant; altogether he was carrying a rather heavy load.

At the house where he roomed, he had four other boys to share two big rooms they rented. For some time the four other boys had been having a lot of fun with John; they found that on some nights John would be restless, would mumble and toss in his sleep, would answer questions if asked, and would even get up and go through certain parts of the day's routine as though he were hypnotized.

One night, however, the boys were startled when John got up, and clad only in his pajamas, left the house and began running. They followed him for over a half mile; he ran barefooted through briers and sand burrs with no evidence of pain; without waking up, he turned around and went back to his room.

Later on, John had two attacks of amnesia, the first one preceded by his *running* away from school and collapsing.

Later developments indicated that John was having a very serious inner conflict over some of the attitudes that his parents manifested towards him, and over his own evaluation of himself.

At that particular time he was not able to meet and solve his problems; the only solution was to run from them, unconsciously, of course. Where the need to run became so urgent, amnesia was the result.

John was able finally to come to grips with his problems and with some help worked out a satisfactory solution to them.

Mary R. was a young widow, left with three small children and some heavy debts, and no insurance. In the adjustment period following when she had to learn to be mother, father and sole support of the children, she maintained a very brave countenance through the day. But at night, she would get up in a sleep-walking condition, get in her car, and drive a long while although always returning home. A relative staying with her first discovered what she was doing and told her of her actions.

Mary R. began to put the car keys in places that she was sure would make them difficult for her to find in her sleep walking; nevertheless, she went on driving and driving and driving. The most rational explanation for her behavior is that she was trying to escape the great burden bearing her down, but always there was something that brought her back.

Later developments in Mary R.'s case indicated that as time the great healer helped her make the adjustment, her night-driving episodes became fewer and fewer until they stopped altogether.

These actual case studies are quoted only as evidence that there is a deep part of each of us, many times hidden, that is very important in our behavior and feelings.

One of the greatest barriers to good mental health is our own low opinions of ourselves.

In the rest of this chapter, we want to discuss how these low opinions generate some of the things we do because of these "inferiority feelings", and how Christianity as a way of life is the perfect panacea for such feelings and the unhappiness they bring.

All neurotics and psychotics are fearful or anxious. This fear is always in some way centered about themselves. They feel inadequate, lacking in the strength and wisdom necessary to meet the problem, and feel that they cannot receive outside help from either God or man. Consequently, as the whole burden is shifted more to their own shoulders, and they are already insecure, they feel more insecure, more helpless, and more hopeless.

Some might say, "The solution is prayer; let them pray." But perhaps those who offer such advice may believe only in the psychological effect of prayer on the one who is praying and do not really believe in a God who answers prayers. It is easily seen that there is little if any psychological effect on one who is praying if he has no faith in the One he is praying to; and if he has a deep, abiding sense of certainty in God and His goodness, he will likely not be in the disturbed condition that we are discussing; hence there will be little need for "emergency prayers".

This one who has the deep, abiding sense of certainty in God and His goodness has always prayed. It is impossible for us to believe in and live in the light of this great, warm, friendly, helpful Personality without talking to Him. So those who believe in Him have always put their problems before Him and have asked Him for advice and help, confident that they will receive it. Such do not have troubles of the mind and emotions except for just the passing moment.

But these who are constantly disturbed have not come yet to this point of belief and dependence; consequently, it is useless to tell them to pray. They first must be taught to believe truly in and depend on this One. When this happens, prayer will be a natural consequence. This teaching concerning the dependence on the One that can always be an ever-present help in time of need should, of course, begin early in life and be an absorbed learning rather than a formal teaching; although formal teaching will certainly reinforce the absorption.

This is not to say that even when one is old he cannot come to have a real faith in God and His help. A person can but it is much harder this way. There are so many habits, teachings, and attitudes that this person has to unlearn before the other, better learning can take effect.

As each one of us goes forward from birth until death, we are forever in the center of the conflict of the within and the without.

From infancy we are conscious of the very strong feelings within ourselves and of the very strong forces of the environment without. We are not conscious as infants or children how the within and the without are interrelated; but as thinking adults, we can appraise this interrelationship intelligently.

For many weeks after we are born our feelings are matters of satisfaction or denial. If we are made to go hungry, to lie uncomfortably, to be swaddled in wet clothing, we feel bad and let the world know it in no uncertain terms. One of our strongest demands is that we be noticed by the other human beings that we have now joined. This noticing comes naturally for most of us, for we have a mother and father, possibly others in the family, who hold us, gurgle at us, bathe us, change us, put us to sleep, wake us up, rock us, pick us up, put us down, and all the time murmur unintelligible baby talk at us that no baby can understand. This noticing is inextricably wrapped up in the affection that others have for us; this affection is as necessary to life as food, water, air and warmth. Strange, isn't it, that a non-physical something is as necessary for life as the physical components?

Nevertheless it is true. Physicians have a term for wasting away and dying from lack of affection and attention that besets so many unwanted children. Marasmus, they call it. And it is a part of the layman's vocabulary today that TLC, a common prescription for children, stands for tender, loving care. There is no synthetic on the market to replace it. And no one can give this prescription to the child as the parents can.

Is it hard to visualize that in four short years of a baby's life, if he is brought up in an atmosphere where he is deficient in TLC, the child soon comes to have an attitude within himself concerning himself that he is a stranger in a foreign land, a derelict on a sea of loneliness? And during these plastic years when the impressions of the without are so strong because they are so new, is it strange that the child crystallizes a feeling or attitude about his relations to others of being unwanted, unneeded, and unnecessary?

We are still infants, really, when the words begin. No one knows just when, how much, and in what way the infant begins to understand words; but by the time the child is from twelve to fifteen months old, we are quite disappointed if he is not making some kind of sounds that we interpret as words. There seems to be little doubt that the child understands the meaning of words long before he is able to use them.

Consider that words have not only an inherent, sometimes many inherent meanings, but in addition have a meaning according to the tone of voice, the inflection of the voice, who says the word, under what circumstances the word is used, what other words are used with the word, and the situation both preceding and containing the use of the word—we can see, considering these things, that the child from the time a sound impinges on his ears begins to associate meaning, or feelings, with words.

As soon as these words begin to make sense to the child, he begins to mold a viewpoint concerning himself based on the meanings of these words. Probably very early in life the child has come to consider himself good or bad, dumb or smart, pretty or ugly, sickly or healthy, a nuisance or a pleasure, forward or shy, talented or untalented, active or lethargic all through the meanings of words that pour in on him from all around. These early self concepts are very important. If a child is loved, he is loved through actions and words. If a child is unwanted and rejected, many times this shows up first in words; nagging, complaining, cursing are excellent ways of projecting attitudes and feelings.

At the same time that the child begins to form a concept, or concepts about himself, largely through the impact of words, he also begins to form a concept or concepts about the world outside himself.

As has been suggested, likely he already has the feeling that it is either a warm, friendly, loving world or a cold, dangerous, hateful world, according to the way he has been received into the family. It is also likely that such feelings will be reinforced and built upon through words and other means as the child grows older; for by words as much as actions we project our true selves.

In this concept of the world outside himself, the child begins to learn from others what seems to be valuable and worth while.

He learns that honesty is the best policy only if those about him prove through their words, actions, and attitudes that honesty is the best policy. He learns that to lie is rewarding if he sees it bringing rewards of some kind to those about him, or if unwise parents or relatives force him into a position where lying brings a reward. This reward may be the absence of punishment.

He learns that such things in the world as furs, expensive cars, ornate houses, elaborate furniture, all the latest gadgets, jewelry, show, pride, pomp, prestige, power, influence are the greatest things in life and greatly desired by many.

He learns of man's inhumanity to man, that injustice is more than an idea, that dishonesty and crookedness may exist in high places, that the race is not always to the swift nor the battle to the strong, that he must get while the getting is good and let the devil take the laggards—that only fools look out for the rights and privileges of others, and the wise man looks out only for himself. He learns these wrong concepts as easily as the right.

Or he learns that pride in oneself is far more worthwhile than the cheers of the crowd, that peace and contentment are among the highest virtues, that love is a force that makes all other combinations of forces look puny, that success cannot be measured by fame, but only by oneself.

He learns that the things of the world which can be touched, tasted, seen, handled, heard, and smelled are but shadows, and that the immaterial things of the spirit of man and God are the substance.

He learns that happiness is not made up of pleasure but of living a constructive life; that man does not live or die to himself but that every aspect and phase of his life must take others into consideration.

He learns, if he is fortunate, that the greatest man is utterly insignificant and that the wisest man is a fool when God is considered. He learns that it is not good for man to walk alone, and in Christianity he can find his friend and confidante. He learns that, like the words of a Latvian religious song, "My God and I go in the fields together, we walk and talk as good friends should and do; we clasp our hands, our voices ring with laughter, My God and I walk through the meadow's hue."

Thus one can establish the bases for mental health.

A few early absorb such attitudes concerning themselves that they may always be off balance emotionally.

But most of us, and this book is directed to the most of us that are called the normal, run into mental health problems because of valuing the wrong things, striving to attain in wrong ways, and thus are preparing to have a certain amount of trouble.

An assumption concerning the functioning of the human personality accepted by nearly all psychologists is that the human being is ego centered, or to put it another way, that the human being is always conscious of self and its relation to the other people and the things round about him.

So it is not at all hard to understand that once we have been taught a scale of values as to what is and what is not important, we always place *ourselves* somewhere on this scale.

"She is pretty, but I am prettier than she is," is one of the applications of this idea that many little girls early learn in life. They cannot believe, because they are not taught, that their beauty is not an absolute thing, but always a relative thing. Regardless of how pretty a little girl might be, she feels some sense of failure if she is constantly made to recognize that another little girl is prettier than she is. So it is not only conceivable, but it happens often, that a pretty little girl comes to think of herself as an ugly little girl, not because she is really ugly, but because she has been led to look on others as being prettier than she is.

We could not investigate this matter very thoroughly without also investigating the concept of "pretty" and "ugly" and how these concepts affect one.

Even in most homes that pride themselves on being Christian homes the physical more often than the Christian definition of beauty is held to; and as long as physical standards of beauty are valued there will be those who are beset with a disturbing sense of failure; some body conformations, despite all the dieting and exercising that might be heaped upon them will never conform to Miss America standards. Some noses, some mouth shapes, some jaw lines, some profiles, some eye colors will never meet the standards that are proclaimed "exquisite" by the connoisseur of beauty. And since in our culture these standards are proclaimed from every publication, every picture tube, every loud speaker, every billboard, and every giant-size screen, it takes exceedingly much of the right kind of teaching to nullify this kind of teaching.

It can be nullified only if a person is one of the rare ones that has been led to pay little attention to outward appearance as being fundamentally worthwhile but instead believes that real beauty is a much deeper thing than physical appearance. First Peter three indicates that real beauty is made up of the hidden person of the heart.

True, some of these qualities of the hidden person of the heart creep into one's physical appearance. For instance the size and the shape of the mouth are matters over which the individual has no control. But the individual does control the way he holds his mouth and with this expressive part of the body he can indicate fear, disapproval, happiness, bitterness, grief, all without saying a word. If bitterness is a fundamental part of the hidden person of the heart, it is more than likely to show up in the way the person manages his mouth— and such a way of management may become habitual.

Most of us have seen persons who have features that are classified as "beautiful" in the grip of some strong and unlovely emotion that contorts their features. Never then are these people beautiful; the classic profile, the well modulated jaw, the fine texture of skin, the sparkling eye—none of these has beauty in the grip of such emotions. Only stark, cruel, raw ugliness shows up then.

Suppose that basically such emotions are the foundations of the "beautiful" person's life. When they are before an admiring audience—and it may be as small as a husband or wife, or as large as thousands—they keep their basic self hidden and bask in their physical beauty and let it shine on their admiring audience. But sooner or later their audiences, large or small, begin to get glimpses of the hidden person of the heart. It is never a pleasant experience.

We as a society must take a part of the blame for such a distorted scale of values.

The emphasis on outward appearance and physical beauty automatically carries with it germs of poor mental health. There can never be anything so physically beautiful but that such beauty can be exceeded and so what was once success now becomes failure. And for those of us who are the ordinary normal ones, failure hurts. Sometimes we withdraw from the competition if we fail enough, and this is not good. Or sometimes we are set on fire to show everybody, and we do—and rarely ever is this good.

All normal people have failed in some respect or another, but always their failures have been few enough and far enough between, and in between there was enough security and feeling of success, that we simply learn not to be hurt too much by failing. Because of this some unthinking persons say: "Failure is good for a child." Never was a bigger lie told in the area of mental health. Some failure, under the right conditions only, acts as an antitoxin. But give a child big doses of antitoxin every day and you kill him.

Thus as long as we emphasize and over-evaluate or worship physical appearance, we are destined to fail where there is no real need to fail.

Age, time, and deterioration are as much a part of the cycle of life and existence as are beginnings and progressions. But many of us have mental health problems because we refuse to recognize not only the inevitable facts that the passing of time brings, but we over-evaluate the worth of that which is at the beginning of the time span rather than the end.

How much to be pitied is the woman well on in years who advertises to the public that she is not at all pleased with being what she is but instead is trying to convince herself by the way she dresses and arranges her hair and her face that she is still in the vigor of young womanhood. She is fooling no one but herself.

How ludicrous is the man who although well over the hill tries to be the gay young blade and thinks he is really a wow with the women! He simpers, he preens, he licks his fur and picks his feathers; he struts and crows and growls and snarls, all for young female consumption, who are not having any at present. It is all well and good that some glamourous male movie stars are on the shady side of fifty—but they have make-up, lighting, and cameras to hide the circles and lines that are superimposed on their naturally aging skins. If said movie star were not a movie star, and circulated sans make-up and build-up, the average young female would not give him a second glance.

These to be pitied old men and old women who refuse to face reality go about their futile ways to make believe they are something they are not and have to suffer the consequences in the realm of mental health.

Beauty is born to die.

In our age and culture we put tremendous premiums on strength, as well as young female physical beauty, and physical vigor. Athletes are heroes, and pages of every newspaper are given over to their doings. Young female beauty has not only pages in newspapers but has whole magazines devoted to it. From every side we are propagandized with the worth, success, and value of such things; it is the unusual person who is somehow given the depth of perception that to look upon such things as being measures of success, is—even though he attains the highest measures himself—doomed to failure.

Each new day's sunrise may see the blossoming of new beauty; but just as the day brings forth the blossom, the succeeding days make sure that this beauty fades. Each new day may see the progressive development of physical strength and vigor, but the succeeding days just as surely reverse the process.

Then these qualities, so highly valued by the world, will bring possessors a sense of failure, for they are predestined to lose them. And if they have valued them highly while possessing them, or if much of their life is built around such things, then their sense of failure and loss is great when time inexorably takes them away. A few of these people do make the proper adjustments, can rebuild their lives on a different basis and live comfortably and happily with themselves. But most who value these things so highly make no such readjustments, and if they live very long, usually lead bitter lives, full of an ever present sense of loss.

These people are not confined to institutions, and these people are not often marked as being among the legion of mentally ill. But their mental health is very, very bad. They are certainly to be classified as chronic invalids.

If instead of over-valuing such things as beauty, strength, wealth, and power in our times and our culture—and what times and cultures have been different?—we instead put a greater value on contentment and peace within and a real Christian relationship with our fellow man, we should have many more mentally healthy people in this great land of ours.

Here would be measures of success that would not be predestined to bring their possessors failure with the passage of time, but instead as the hours and months melt into years and centuries, the measure of success would be heightened and strengthened.

Here would be measures of success that could make mankind look forward to the passing of the years rather than looking to them with dread.

Here would be measures of success wherein no measure of failure could be applied from others and from without.

Here would be measures of success that could almost carry a built in guarantee; for where beauty, strength, wealth, and power are measures of success there must be striving and stressful living in ways that are detrimental to the personality involved. Where contentment and peace within and Christian relationships with our fellow man are the measures of success, these are attained without striving and stressful living, and the very absence of most strife and stress bring both success and mental health.

This is not to say that all striving and stress are harmful to mental health, for they are not. Man will always struggle with his natural environment to wrest a living from it and improve it, and this struggle is good for mental health, not bad. Man will always be under a certain amount of stress because of this struggle, and he will always undergo times of stress because of his concern for the ones he loves. But practically never does a psychologist or a psychiatrist deal with a person who is highly disturbed because he *actually* is concerned about others. The disturbed person may say this and such a situation may seem to be a symptom of the malady, but practically never is such a situation at the bottom of the disturbed person's trouble. The disturbed person is virtually always disturbed about himself.

Outward symbols carry a great wealth of meaning. By symbols that others see we tell what we are like inside.

Through blocks of stone men have tried to gain immortality, worship God, and crystallize feeling. In no case have they been successful, but they still try, sure that they have succeeded.

By means of fine clothes and furs, elaborate houses, sparkling jewels, and expensive cars men proclaim to their fellow men that they occupy a higher plane than does another man. Such things that give them "prestige" and "status" in the eyes of these others are strong meat to their egos. If all were to believe that a cloth coat is as good as a fur coat, one thing we know—fur coats would cost no more than cloth coats. If all were to believe that a house is for inside living and not for outside showing, we could find no twenty room mansions for two lonely old people. If all were to believe that cars are for transportation and not for the "ohs" and "ahs" they elicit, fewer of us would try to brag by means of the automobile sitting in our driveway.

Through physical means we try to meet the requirements of the without and thus set the standards for the within. If a fine car, a fine house, and a fine coat can bring admiration to the faces of others that we can plainly see, then within we come to value such things highly and begin to shape our lives around the core of such values. Within we burn, and motivate and drive ourselves to achieve the things without that others can admire.

These things that are without may not be always physical; they can be such things as position, fame, honor, acclaim, prestige, status, and various achievements of a tangible sort that are visible to others.

Thus our lives come to be geared not to a set of values that we have set up for ourselves but geared to a set of values that others around us set up for us, and in turn each of these has his set of values set up for him by those around him.

To be horribly blunt about the matter, we live in a time and a culture when force is more admired than gentleness, where might is the accepted way rather than right, where possessions and not serenity of life mark one as a success, where sensuality is much more boldly acclaimed and promoted than sensitivity—we live such that man's thought processes have so degenerated that we believe security comes from without and not from within. We have daily dinned into us that these things outside—bonds, money, savings, power of government, military might, insurance and retirement programs, Social Security, educational degrees, professional status can make us secure.

But security is not something we have, security is something we are. Death, disease, and decay will creep into the most strongly fortified keep; a coalition of all the presidents, premiers, and emperors of the earth cannot put the tiniest guarantee upon tomorrow. The earth is only an atom in a great chain of universal molecules and man is not even an electron in the atom.

We are such fools to believe that security can be built up around us, bit by bit, like a mason building a brick house while enclosing himself within!

It is not so.

Then what?

A feeling of security, which is basic to good mental health, is a matter of the spirit and not of physical things. Being a matter of the spirit, and man being a spiritual being, it follows that this feeling of security is a part of the within and not a part of the without.

Without money or guarantee of the future, one who believes that God is on his side can feel secure.

Without public accclaim or favor, one who is living a life that satisfies himself and who believes that it satisfies his God can have a deep sense of well being.

With no backing of force or display of threat one may still be sure that love is the greatest power and will take him farther than either threat or force.

With no fame or blaring publicity or glaring headlines one may go about humble tasks that may be even menial and monotonous, and yet have a deeper sense of something accomplished than a cabinet member.

God, who made man, and who does not ask a team of psychologists, psychiatrists, physicians, social workers, and professors how man operates, knows what makes the good life.

He inspired His Son as He walked the earth in the flesh to say in Matthew five that blessed are the poor in spirit, those who mourn, the meek, those who hunger and thirst for righteousness, the merciful, the pure in heart, the peacemakers, and those who are persecuted and reviled for righteousness' sake.

Not one of these blessings is material or is acquired and held as a possession; not one of these blessings is held in very high esteem by the world.

But all of these blessings are a part of the good life, and as we learn a little more each day about the meaning of each blessing, and see how that it brings good and not evil to our lives, we come more fully to comprehend that the Christian life is the abundant life—that it is the way to a life of mental health that makes the wheezing, halting theorizings of myopic man show up for the feeble efforts that they are.

CHAPTER IX

More than Conquerors

In Romans eight there is one of the greatest truths in all the Bible, yes, in all the world, to firm up our foundations of security, to bolster our feelings of inner certainty.

"If God is for us, who is against us? He who did not spare his own Son but gave him up for us all, will he not also give us all things with him? Who shall bring any charge against God's elect? It is God who justifies; who is to condemn? Is it Christ Jesus, who died, yes who was raised from the dead, who is at the right hand of God, who indeed intercedes for us? Who shall separate us from the love of Christ? Shall tribulation, or distress, or persecution, or famine, or nakedness, or peril, or sword? As it is written: 'For thy sake we are being killed all the day long; we are regarded as sheep to be slaughtered.' No, in all these things we are more than conquerors through him who loved us. For I am sure that neither death, nor life, nor angels, nor principalities, nor things present, nor things to come, nor powers, nor height, nor depth, nor anything else in all creation will be able to separate us from the love of God in Christ Jesus our Lord."

As the human life progresses we realize more and more our own needs; needs that must be supplied partly from within ourselves, and partly from outside ourselves. The help that God gives us and the help that our fellows give us come from without, but both have a profound effect upon us and influence the kind of help we can give ourselves within.

No man is sufficient unto himself.

When we are in the grip of some great emotional turbulence and suffering intensely, only then do we fully realize how much we need someone to help. Fortunate is the one who can talk to his Father and Elder Brother and realize in full measure why the prophets of old spoke of Christ as "counselor." Fortunate is the one who has husband, wife, mother, father, friends who can listen and help without taking over the person's life and begin shoving this way and that.

Sigmund Freud, one of the central figures of modern psychology, was one of those who could act as counselor but could find no counselor in return. He was Jewish by birth, but because of the materialism of the age had rejected the God of his people. In his book on *Moses and Monotheism* Freud states his case, and we are made to pity him. He says that he envies those who have a simple and trusting faith in God because life is so much simpler for them than for people like himself!

How many untold millions alive today are casting about they know not where; they only know that they are wandering, forlorn, and undone! Since man is fated to lose himself in something, these to be pitied millions lose themselves in wars, intrigues, plays for power, amassing things of material value, competing with one another for beauty, popularity, and prestige, or pleasure, drunkeness, and dope addiction—the byways where they can lose themselves are legion. Finally many of these come to lose themselves within themselves and truly these are lost souls while they yet live.

Then there are the fortunate who early or late have come to realize that their own power, wisdom, worthwhileness, and goodness depend a great deal on their attitudes— attitudes of firm belief that God is their ever present help in time of need. These are the realistic ones who know that they are not always self-sufficient; but they know that if they do their best, God is always on their team, and He will do the rest.

These are not persons who use prayer only as an emergency measure or a Sunday exercise, but these are persons who as they walk along whatever way is their lot to walk, walk hand in hand with God—although they may not see around the curves in the road ahead, they know that way has been well marked by their Christ, and they are secure with the feeling that they will not falter, stumble, or get lost.

Too, these fortunate ones recognize that since man is fated to lose himself in something, one of the best ways in which he can lose himself is the welfare of his fellow man, made in the image of God.

This losing of oneself in others begins at home and first must include our relations with our nearest and dearest. But from home base this relation must spread, as it has opportunity, to all men. This losing of oneself in others is simply called "love" in the New Testament. "How can we love God, whom we have not seen, and not love our fellow man (made in the image of God) whom we have seen?" we are forced to ask ourselves by the words of the Spirit of God. Thus we are made to see that the love of God in one's heart is not a theoretical idea, not a shadowy, immaterial concept, but a truth that is based on something demonstrable—the love we bear toward our fellow man. Regardless of what our mouthings might be as to our love for our fellow man, our actions show the yes or the no of it. It is here that begins the love of God and here that begins the great losing of ourselves in others that is the great loss and the great gain. "Whoever loses his life will preserve it."

As we grow older so often our lives become of narrowing focus rather than broadening, of inward turning interests rather than outward.

By the time we have reached adolescence we have become afraid to be an individual; one might say that the overwhelming desire of the average adolescent is to "be like the gang." By the time we are in our thirties most of us have developed a shell of habits, thoughts, and interests that seem to offer security of a sort, and we are afraid to attempt anything that might crack this shell and let something new in. By the time we have passed middle age, most of us are so intent on maintaining the status quo that it is no wonder the world has come to believe the great untruth that "you can't teach an old dog new tricks."

Why are we like this?

Because we are afraid. We are afraid of death, and principalities, things present and things to come, of powers, of height and depth and things of creation both known and unknown. In short we are afraid of life and seek just to exist, filling our bellies and seeking some kind of guarantee that they will continue to be filled, trying to make sure that we keep our bodies warmed and clothed, striving to maintain our "status" among others, whatever that is, and willing to use almost any means, including violence itself, to achieve these so-called "desirable" ends.

The one who knows that God is for him is not afraid. He has become more than a conqueror. These puny obstacles of the world have been soundly bounced around and are now laid in front of this triumphant personality to be used as stepping stones. This one has now become explorer and investigator with all of life and eternity stretching before him.

He is not afraid of the present because God is at his side. He is not afraid of things to come because God will be there to help him where he cannot help himself. He is not afraid of principalities or powers with their threat of violence, death, and taxes over him, for God will help him to be wiser than they. He is not afraid of the depths of Sheol or the heights of the unlimited universe because his friend, his father, his God is there.

Having conquered fear through the help of God, he is ready and eager to live each day of life as it comes to him, knowing that each day is different from every other day, that life in its progression from birth to death is a part of a perfect whole. This one has no regrets at being young or old or at whatever stage or lot in life he finds himself because all is well; God is his helper.

This one asks no mortgage of the future; it is enough to leave that in God's hands.

This one asks no guarantees of physical security, for his faith in God has given him all the security that he needs.

This one does not ask or demand an escape from tribulations, distress, persecution, famine, nakedness, peril, or even the atomic sword because he knows that if these come to him, they come for a reason that finally will help him and not hurt him, and that they last but through a fleeting moment of eternity. Even if they should result in his physical death, they have not really harmed him but only sooner have released him to live perfectly and completely.

None of these things cause the one who believes in the unswerving love of God through His Son to be sad or unhappy or fearful. This one who believes in this love is not forced to grub his way through the beggarly elements of a material minded world, for he knows that the physical things of life are only a means to an end, not intrinsically valuable, to be used and forgotten for the relatively valueless trivia that they are.

This one knows that life is for the living, not the getting.

This one is happy, content with what he has, not anxious about the morrow.

This one loves and is loved in return.

This one is unenvious, not covetous, for he takes God's scale of values.

This one is serene, even though in pain—hopeful, although dying—secure, although penniless. For he knows that if God is for him, he cannot escape His great love shown to him in all circumstances through Jesus Christ His Son.

Surely this one is more than a conqueror, for having conquered all these things that beset and befog the mind, soul, and spirit of the earthbound man, he can go on in the great adventure of living, always reaching new heights and new vistas that will be limited only by the nonexistent limits of eternity itself.

Truly—he *is* more than conqueror.

CHAPTER X

Think on these Things

The majority of persons are swayed by feelings rather than by mind, although some of those that are most swayed would be the first and the loudest to deny it. There is something that they desire very much, that is of great value in their lives. They bend every energy to reach this goal. If they should be questioned either by others or by themselves, they rationalize and give what seem to be good, logical reasons for their actions. Actually they are participating in the oldest of human faults, the shaping of their thoughts to fit their feelings.

The average individual is a mass of "yes, but's."

The "yes, but" device is another way for one to dodge reality. And the dodging of reality is not good for one's mental health. Christianity is a religion of facing reality. "You shall know the truth, and the truth shall make you free."

Mental health can never be achieved by our kidding ourselves, or by attempting to kid others. A deception can go so far but no farther. Finally we feel, even though we do not intellectually recognize, that something is wrong, and this unconscious realization that we are at cross purposes with ourselves bubbles and boils within us and may make us uncomfortable at the least and psychotic at the most. As an example the New Testament is full of teachings about the dangers of riches and of wanting to be rich. But take the average group of college students, steeped in the culture of our present day world, and present to them the idea that the desire to be rich is a snare and a delusion. Most will likely agree in the following manner: "Well, of course that's true, but ...."

Present the Christian idea that love is a greater force than violence. "Certainly, that's the ideal situation, but ...."

Set forth the Biblical teaching that a man should return good for evil. "Yes, that's all very well, but ....".

These are all illustrations of the fact that our minds will agree with such statements, but that our feelings will dictate our actions.

Christianity emphasizes the control of our feelings through our intellect. Today in the world this is practically an unknown quantity. Psychotherapeutic devices today practically never start with an intellectual approach. No psychologist or psychiatrist would think of saying at first to a disturbed client: "Your problem is purely a matter for the intellect to solve. Let's put down here, one, two, three, the things that you do that bring about the results that are so disturbing to you. Then you can eliminate the cause, and the effect disappears."

Finally, of course, this very thing has to happen if the client is to be helped—but he has to arrive at this insight himself, with the psychologist or psychiatrist treading very softly, and indirectly, to help him arrive at such conclusions. Sometimes the process of getting to the intellectual functions through the emotional approach will take months, even years.

Where can the intellect be brought to bear, then, to help man in his seeking after emotional stability?

The answer is fairly obvious.

If the intellect is used on an emotional and psychological problem in between the times before the problem, or problems, are most severe, then some progress will be made.

It is in between times, when we are not so much in the grip of the emotion, that we can come nearest facing reality concerning the whole situation. We can do even better if we can put the problem into words; this is hardly ever done except in the presence of another person.

So often our most severe problems concern our feelings about ourselves; feelings of guilt and inadequacy. Or to put it another way, our faults. "Confess your sins to one another" is an admonition of the New Testament and "Judge not that you be not judged", is another.

Herein are two of the main foundations of the constructive work that the counseling psychologist and the psychiatrist can do.

The counselor listens to one putting his faults into words. The counselor listens as a sympathetic friend whose emotions are not overly involved in the problem. He passes no judgment and does not try to dominate or dictate the life of the person with the problem; he simply serves as one who can help the problem ridden one come to a new viewpoint and achieve a new insight into his own motivations, faults, and feelings.

To the person with a problem the reactions and attitudes of those close to him may be representative of the way he sees the reactions and attitudes of the world about him. A child reared in a very critical home expects to find and does in his own feelings, a very critical world. A young person who is taught to be utterly dependent on those about him in the home may continue to be utterly dependent on those nearest to him when he leaves home. He carries with him these extreme feelings of dependence. A child who is forever being frustrated and made to feel highly aggressive may carry this spirit of aggressiveness with him wherever he goes, as long as he lives.

Attitudes, feelings, ideas can change, of course. This would be a sorry world if they could not. When our attitudes, feelings, and ideas make us uncomfortable, they may become uncomfortable enough that we want to change them. For persons who are having psychological and emotional problems, the first step in solving them is becoming so uncomfortable with them that they feel that some new step must be taken. Herein the counselor, whether psychologist, psychiatrist, minister, physician, teacher, or whoever, can play a great part in helping this person to help himself. For it takes at least one other person to help us lift ourselves from the sloughs of emotion that lie all about on the map of life. No one can do it alone. "No man is an island."

The principles of Christianity when applied to an individual's life are completely effective. They will not and cannot be applied by the average individual unless he has more than verbal teaching concerning them. Besides hearing them he must have both the opportunity to absorb them and to put them to work for himself.

The child reared in the Christian home will have the love and affection needed for future emotional stability, for these are fundamental in Christian living.

Fear in its destructive aspects is conquered for the Christian. Death, the greatest fear and the greatest unknown, is wiped out. The worst that the world can have to offer is insignificant, for God is on the Christian's side.

People, for the Christian, are not enemies but friends, for God is love, and is not man made in God's image? And even though some of these people may act little, ugly, and mean, and may even set themselves up as the Christian's enemies for a while, such a state cannot last, for the Christian does not consider them as enemies but as people to be loved. And enmity does not do well under such conditions.

Security, in both its inner and outward aspects, is taken care of for the Christian. God has promised him that if he will seek His righteousness all these necessary things will be added unto him; and since God is his father, knowing all about him and what he does, this one always feels inwardly secure, like the little child who has been tucked in by loving hands for the night.

The world and its people are not a threat to the Christian. The Christian does not labor under a great burden of inferiority, for he recognizes that success, attainment, and real stature in life are not a matter between him and other men but a matter between himself and his God. He knows that God does not see labels but instead sees lives.

The Christian knows but may not understand how it is that there is ultimate purpose and ultimate good. And since he is a small part of all of this, then in his life too there is ultimate purpose and ultimate good.

For the Christian all will be well, despite whatever problems and disappointments he may have.

As Paul admonished the Philippians, "Finally, brethren, whatever is true, whatever is honorable, whatever is just, whatever is pure, whatever is lovely, whatever is gracious, if there is any excellence, if there is anything worthy of praise, think about these things."

Date Due

NOV 3			
NOV 15			
NOV 19			
OCT 1			
MAR 9 1981			
MAR 2 5 1981			
ILL/RH 8/30/90			
AUG 1 5 '90			
AG 9 '94			
MAY 16 '95			
MAY 2 9 1997			
MAR 1 5 '98			
	PRINTED	IN U. S. A.	